No. 1423
$17.95

THE COMPLETE BOOK OF
HOME
COMPUTERS

BY VAN WATERFORD

TAB BOOKS Inc.
BLUE RIDGE SUMMIT, PA. 17214

FIRST EDITION

FIRST PRINTING

Copyright © 1982 by TAB BOOKS Inc.

Printed in the United States of America

Reproduction or publication of the content in any manner, without express permission of the publisher, is prohibited. No liability is assumed with respect to the use of the information herein.

Library of Congress Cataloging in Publication Data

Waterford, Van.
    The complete book of home computers.

    Includes index.
    1. Minicomputers. 2. Microcomputers. I. Title.
QA76.5.W357 1982   001.64   82-5850
ISBN 0-8306-2423-6   AACR2
ISBN 0-8306-1423-0 (pbk.)

30124 75152 42061

JACK PALMER

31-12-81

Contents

Ohio Scientific Inc. (OSI)—Quasar—Panasonic—Personal Micro Computers—Radio Shack—RCA (Single-Board)—Rockwell International (Single-Board)—Sinclair Research Ltd.—Texas Instruments Inc.

Introduction

30124 75152 42061

JACK PALMER

31-12-81

This book was written with you, the user, in mind. "Home computers" have not captured the market yet as have video cassette recorders and other such devices, but the time will soon arrive when they will be considered just another home appliance.

That it hasn't happened yet is largely due to the fact that whatever computer system you buy, you still have to press keys on a keyboard and do some sort of programming in order to get some satisfaction out of the system.

Perhaps you want to wait until "voice recognition" has been perfected in such a way that, after plugging the system in, you just tell the computer "verbally" what you want it to do. Well, that is still a few years off.

Why not then try pressing some keys. I had fun doing so with the computer system loaned to me by Ohio Scientific Inc. "Big deal," you might say, "You didn't have to pay for it."

Well, let me say, that although my many writing assignments actually don't afford me the time, I am in the process of acquiring a single-board computer. This way I can program the system from A to Z to do what I want it to do.

Why don't you try it. This book describes so many systems on the market, that after careful reading, you should be able to choose the system that best fits you.

Good luck!

Part 1
Overview

Chapter 1
Home Information
Systems

While it would be premature to describe the computer as a common household appliance, forecasts indicate that it will not be long before home computer sales exceed one million units a year. By 1985, sales of home computers are expected to reach millions of computers a year. Thirty million American homes will be wired for cable, and 7.5 million homes will have two-way cable. This wired "home of the future" will include such wonders as electronic newspapers, a virtually limitless selection of video entertainment, and facilities for teleshopping, home banking, and centralized control of energy and home appliances.

Experts feel that such major sociological changes as the increase in the number of working women, various economic upheavals, and the energy crisis are creating a demand for more computerized products. This means that the explosion in the use of computers for personal (home) use has just begun: what started, years ago, as a hobby market, has now become a major consumer product.

The potential of the home computer is enormous. Among the possible applications are: games, education (learning devices), home-energy monitoring, home security, appliance control, bookkeeping, control of medical devices, and—perhaps most exciting—the recasting of the home as an information center, providing everything from the latest news to the availability of airline tickets . . . from stock market tips to the latest department-store bargains!

Just how soon the computer will become a household item depends on many factors, such as the crucial area of component standardization. The average consumer's lack of understanding is certainly another important factor. This book was written to help solve this particular problem. Once you realize that a computer is actually easy to use, you'll be both ready and able to handle other problems.

HOME COMPUTERS TODAY

Probably without being aware of it, you—and almost everyone else in the U.S.—may already use some kind of computer every day. Here are a couple of examples:

● In the computer-controlled Singer sewing machine, the computer controls the frequency and travel of the needle vertically, the position of the needle to the left or right of its center line, and the forward and backward movement of the fabric. In addition, the user can, using the same computer control, select from 27 stitch patterns.

● Many late-model television sets—RCA, Magnavox, Zenith, Sony, GE, and others—use computer-controlled tuner functions.

● Electronic touch-operated controls are used on many microwave and countertop ovens; on dishwashers and laundry equipment; and in heating/cooling systems.

In some versions of the microwave oven, the computer's memory not only starts and stops the cooking at a "time or temperature" signal, but also makes necessary adjustments during the cooking process. One Litton oven, for example, has a vocabulary of 6,000 words! If the code for roast beef is inserted, for example, the computer responds with a voice that inquires as to "Pounds?" and "How done?" Computer-controlled dishwashers not only signal the phase of operation, but can also be preset as much as nine hours before the wash cycle is actually to begin, so that washing can be scheduled for low-energy consumption periods, such as the middle of the night.

SOLID-STATE ELECTRONICS

Almost anything that has cycles and sequences can be computer-controlled—i.e., controlled by pushing buttons. The computer delivers speed and convenience, and we needn't be embarrassed by it. It has nothing to do with laziness: using computers is simply a fast, efficient way to get things done.

What makes all of this possible is the fantastic world of solid-state electronics—*integrated circuits* (ICs), including fingernail-size computer *chips* with hundreds and even thousands of electronic components on them. (A chip is a very small slice of semiconductor material, usually silicon, on which electronic components are grouped. "Very small" means, typically, less than ¼-inch square and 1/1000-inch thick.) Single-chip microcomputers that accept signals from sensors (indicating, for example, temperature, moisture, etc.) are preprogrammed for timing, counting, display, and other controls required in microwave ovens, dishwashers, clothes washers, dryers, and other appliances.

The sensing, monitoring, and control capabilities that integrated circuits provide have extended computer control to other appliances, such as blenders and food processors. In addition, such electronic toys as the trademarked products Simon and Super Simon, are basically computer-controlled toys. And the vacuum fluorescent displays in

4

the Mark VI Lincoln Continental and other automobiles are powered by a microcomputer.

Many of the telephones available in "phone stores" use computer control, and specialized computer controls are used in thermostats, burglar alarms, smoke detectors, and other such items. Some health and exercise machines are equipped with computer-controlled devices, able to accept input on such variables as age, sex, and weight, and to provide feedback on the user's heart range, blood pressure, exercise points gained, calories spent, and so forth. And finally, many workers today use video display terminals at their jobs—in offices, airline terminals, banks, insurance companies, or wherever.

SOFTWARE

According to researchers, in a few years practically all home computers will be able to function as "terminals"—that is, they will be able to access data bases, communicate with other computers and, generate new levels of information for use in everyday human activities.

With the development of more sophisticated *software*—the programs that run computers—the personal/home computer will become more user-oriented, allowing even the very inexperienced to use it. The trend can already be discerned in the design of both *hardware* (the physical components of a computer) and software that is unintimidating, reliable, versatile, attractive, and easily integrated into the home environment.

Through data communications, the "electronic cottage" of the not too far distant future will have access to a wide assortment of information: at-home shopping and banking through a simple terminal; enhanced voice, textual, and facsimile communications; computational power, through ever more versatile home computers; educational devices employing microprocessors and video technology; and an almost endless array of auxiliary services to facilitate life's day-to-day tasks.

One interesting trend is the establishment of a number of home-information services throughout the nation. Recent developments with television-based and telephone-based home-information services suggest that U.S. communications organizations are about to catch up with their counterparts in Great Britain, France, Germany, and Canada, who have so far dominated the market. These home-information systems are important because they are in many respects the forerunners of home computer installations and can be related to them.

HOME INFORMATION

What exactly is home information? It refers to a system of communicating that serves multiple users employing a variety of electronic equipment, such as keyboards, terminals, graphic displays, computers, and the like. Using a home-information system, users can shop electronically, purchasing goods from remote retail outlets; travelers can book reserva-

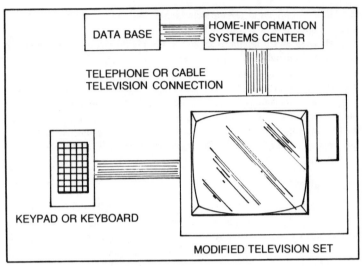

Fig. 1-1. Basic home-information system.

tions; and investors can buy and sell stocks and other securities. In other words, it offers the user both entertainment and such nonentertainment services as information retrieval, messaging, computation, and remote monitoring and control.

Basically, a home-information service consists of two principals: a systems operator and a service provider. The systems operator—whether a telecommunications company, cable company, or TV network—is concerned with the design and coordination of computer/transmission systems; the running of computer centers; providing telecommunication links; and establishing guidelines for service providers. Service providers are companies that have information or transactions to sell—for example, retail stores, catalog, publishers, travel agencies, new services, and security and alarm companies.

Figure 1-1 illustrates the basic concept of a home-information system. A more elaborate view of the system is shown in Fig. 1-2.

Typical Systems

Videotext. This two-way system (Fig. 1-3) typically utilizes a *standard telephone line* to establish a two-way link from the viewer to the data base. This interactive capability allows greater viewer control over an almost infinitely expandable data source. The essential elements of a Videotext system are:

● A computer with a capacity of many thousands, or even millions, of pages of information.

● Computer software that permits rapid retrieval of information and customer billing.

6

● Transmission lines to provide two-way communication between the computer and the customer.

● Display terminals, with accompanying decoder and keyboard (or other retrieval device).

Teletext. This system uses *broadcasting* to disseminate information. It can be a one-way system (Fig. 1-4) or a two-way system. In the latter, *a two-way system* program is piped into the home via coaxial cable on 6 to 12 channels. It can also take the form of a pay-television system, in which particular channels or programs are available for extra charges. Teletext can also be a subscription television system (STV), a form of special pay

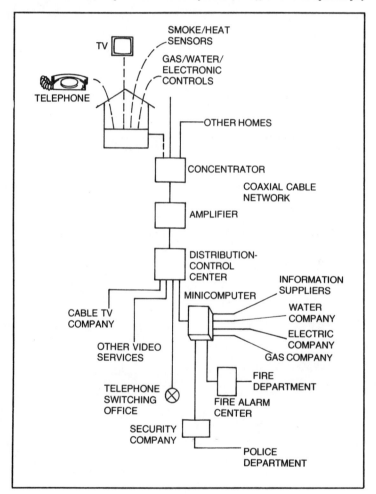

Fig. 1-2. Basic overview of some of the services available with a home-information system.

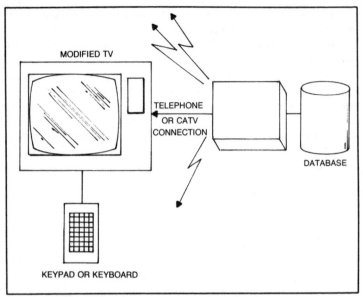

Fig. 1-3. Videotext interactive home-information system.

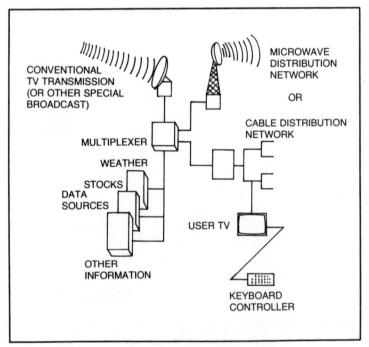

Fig. 1-4. Basic Teletext one-way home-information system.

Table 1-1. Delivery Technologies

System	Delivery Technique			Display Device		Input Device	
	Phone Line	Cable TV	FM Broadcast TV	Home TV	Home Computer	Special Keypad	Alphanumeric Keyboard
Cabletext		X		X			
CompuServe	X				X		X
Cox		X		X		X	
Datacast			X		X		X
Green Thumb	X			X		X	
OCLC	X			X		X	
QUBE		X		X	X*	X	
The Source	X				X		X
Viewtron	X			X		X	

*Not part of basic service but can be added.

programming in which programs are directly beamed to rooftop antennas from a satellite. (It should be noted that Teletext is basically a one-way system, meaning that it's noninteractive.)

DELIVERY SYSTEMS

With regards to home-information delivery, there are questions concerning both the manner of delivery and the devices to be used by the customer (or user). Within the U.S. four delivery approaches are being scrutinized, some of which are already in existence: Over-the-air broadcast provides one-way information: co-axial cable broadcast also provides one-way information. On the other hand, both telephone network-based television systems and home computers provide two-way interactive information.

U.S. Systems

Table 1-1 lists the various U.S. home-information delivery systems.

Cabletext. This one-way Teletext system uses special decoders to receive information from certain service providers.

Cox Cable/Home Service. This two-way system is based on cable television lines. A 20-button keypad is used for interactive communications.

Datacast. A two-way system, Datacast utilizes FM frequencies not currently being used by radio stations. The subscriber needs both a radio receiver and a home computer.

Green Thumb. This computer-based data service supplies farmers with timely facts and forecasts. A Videotext service, it allows users to draw on information stored in data-base computers and display it instantly on a video screen. The terminals have numeric keypads, with additional symbol keys available for use as commands (such as "Display the next page of stored information"). Information that can be "dialed up" in this manner includes future prices, price chart trends, Washington and other political news, market strategy and tactics, and—preeminently—the weather, giving the farmer the accurate, up-to-date information so crucial to his livelihood.

OCLC. Another one-way system, using a special keypad.

QUBE. This is probably the most widely publicized delivery system in the nation. This two-way interactive system from Warner Communications made history in connection with President Carter's address to the people on energy in July, 1979. Ohio QUBE subscribers were able to respond to the President's proposals "live." Using a special numeric keypad, subscribers registered their reactions to five questions asked by *Prime Time Sunday* host Tom Snyder. The era of talking back to television, meaning the end of passive viewing, had arrived!

Today, QUBE III is being used—a keypad (Fig. 1-5) that supports eight numeric digits of data of variable length to and from the terminal, allowing a variety of home-service applications. These include home financial management, teleshopping, security operations, information retrieval, pay-per-view programming, and *narrowcasting*. QUBE III also permits open-ended response (instead of limited multiple-choice selection).

Fig. 1-5. Special keypad used in QUBE III

By adding a home computer, this service gives subscribers access to electronic editions of *The New York Times* and *Washington Post*, in addition to a wealth of other information. (See Fig. 1-6.) By typing in a special code, the user may select the information of his choice to appear on the screen. The additional keypad (Fig. 1-7) allows the subscriber to interact with special narrowcast programs.

Figure 1-8 shows a family participating in a special program; it could be an interactive game, an educational test, or an opinion registration of some kind. The QUBE system provides a gradual way of getting used to operating a home computer.

Viewtron. This experimental two-way interactive service is currently in use in Florida, a joint effort of Knight-Ridder Publications and AT&T. The system provides for continually updated news, weather, sports, stock market quotations, interactive shopping and banking details, travel and entertainment calendars, learning aids, games, quizzes, consumer advice, and energy tips. There are 14 information providers and 17 advertisers. Using a special keypad, the subscriber can, for example, request a list of local restaurants, follow that by a list of only the French restaurants, say, and narrow down that selection to the day's menu in the dining room of his choice. Also, the subscriber can use his interactive device to order anything from a catered dinner to a lawn mower—from a hair dryer to a theater ticket!

Taking a look again at Table 1-1, you can see that there are only three *basic* systems where a home computer is used: CompuServe, Datacast, and

Fig. 1-6. QUBE Videotext system using terminal, computer, and special keypad.

Fig. 1-7. Accessing information through the QUBE Videotext two-way system.

The Source. We'll conclude this section on U.S. delivery systems with an examination of two of them.

CompuService. This service aims its efforts at a broad base of individual users. Offerings include a national bulletin board, lists of users, program packages, special features, games, text editors, software distribution exchange, utilities, and a number of programming languages. The company—located at 5000 Arlington Centre Road, Columbus, OH 43220; telephone (614) 457-8600—sells its services through Radio Shack stores and bases its charges on per-minute usage of phone lines (to gain access to the computer base).

The Source. This property of Source Telecomputing Corp.—1616 Anderson Road, McLean, VA 22102; telephone (703) 821-6660—is a telecomputing network that gives the home-computer user access to literally thousands of programs and data bases. Included is the ability to communicate electronically with other computer users, both interactively and through the exchange of electronic mail. The user can access news, sports, financial, travel, and consumer data bases.

To use The Source, you switch on your computer, turn on your *modem* (a device that lets your computer talk to other computers over the telephone), and pick up your phone. You then dial the nearest number in the Telenet Telephone Access list that comes with your Source documentation. You put the handset on the modem and conduct a dialogue with the automated interrogator at the other end.

One of the most exciting features of The Source is the group of *real-time* data bases available to you when you have a home computer. (*Real-time* refers to live, present-tense action, as distinguished from "canned" data.) These data bases include information on virtually all U.S. and foreign markets for stocks, bonds, gold, silver, and commodities. The Source also provides access to UPI (United Press International) wire service, letting you research the data base for current stories by keywords.

Fig. 1-8. Subscriber family enjoying the QUBE two-way system.

Fig. 1-9. The ideal interactive system, developed by The Source and CompuServe, uses a home computer and modem.

To use a computer and modem rented from The Source, you don't have to be an expert computer user. And by adding a printer, you can exchange electronic mail with other computer users. (The printer is used to permanently store the information.) You can play games, tune in educational programs—the list is practically endless.

If you want to get the latest news on President Reagan, say, you simply sign on (through a local phone call, providing the system with your identification number and private password); type UPI into your terminal; and press the Return key. The system will respond by asking you what type of news you want. If you type PRESIDENT REAGAN onto the screen, the system will respond with a list of stories about the President that day, and ask you whether you want to read forward, read backward, or simply scan the stories. To scan the stories backward in time, you'd type SB, press the Return key; this lets you see the first paragraph only of each story. You may ask the system to give you any complete story by pressing the Break key and giving the appropriate story number. Once you have read the story (or printed it on your printer), you can sign off by typing Quit, Off and pressing the Return key. The system will disconnect and tell you how much time you used (and the cost thereof).

Fig. 1-9 shows a family enjoying the kind of home-computer communications provided by The Source and CompuServe.

Foreign Videotext Services

The U.S. is lagging behind the rest of the world in the development of Videotext services (services without home computers). These foreign services are called, variously: Prestel (Great Britain); Teletel or Antiope (France); Bildschirmtext (West Germany); Captains (Japan); Telidon (Canada); and Telset (Finland). We'll look at developments in two foreign countries in some detail.

Great Britain. Teletext began in the United Kingdom in 1976. There are two versions—CEEFAX, serviced by the nationalized British Broadcasting Company (BBC); and ORACLE, serviced by the commercial television network. Called Prestel, the system has a number of capabilities reflecting its two-way interactive character. Game playing against the system is available, as is a simple electronic mail service. Anyone can be a service provider for the system. The British Postoffice (PTT), for example, has already demonstrated Prestel in some 20 countries, including Russia and certain Far and Middle Eastern countries. West Germany, Switzerland, The Netherlands, and Hong Kong have also subscribed to Prestel. However, at a cost of $2,000 each (for terminal and accessories), public acceptance has been slow.

The Prestel network uses a series of distributed viewdata-center computers, each containing the same replicated data bases. The BPO operates the videotext centers as well as the telephone lines but exercises no control over the contents of the data bases. It is responsible, however, for maintaining the index to the data base and for ensuring reliable access. (See Fig. 1-10.)

France. The French spearheaded a technological revolution in telecommunications to make the telephone the fundamental component of a comprehensive information-based society. To reach their goal, the French substantially improved their domestic telephone system while launching a

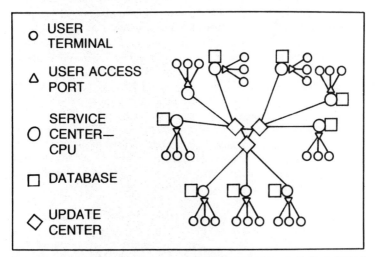

Fig. 1-10. The British Videotext system, Prestel, is based on multiple replicated data bases.

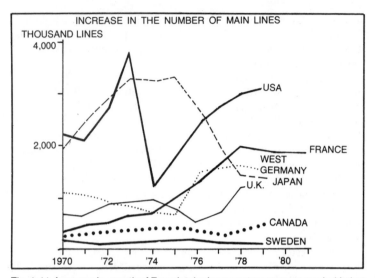

Fig. 1-11. Increase in growth of French telephone system as compared with that of other countries.

far-reaching "telematique" program that combines the capabilities of tele-communications and data processing (known in France as "informatique"). This *telematique* program incorporates telephones, television, *facsimiles* (devices with which to transmit *hard copy*—computer output in printed form— over telephone lines), computer terminals and other media into a harmonious network that permits data and other forms of information to be speedily tranferred. Figure 1-11 illustrates the enormous development of the French phone system compared to that of other countries.

According to French experts, mass computerization will take hold, becoming as indispensable to French society as electricity. And certainly the capabilities of the *telematique* program, using uniform terminals and improved transmission techniques, are vast: written messages and electronic mail can be transmitted between individual subscribers; information may be obtained through a one-way teletext system using a simple keyboard; data processing can be conducted on a compatible interactive Videotext system; and a standard terminal can be used to obtain telephone numbers. This *telematique* program, using the telephone and television as building blocks, allows for the simple hookup of every telephone subscriber to virtually any information source. (See Fig. 1-12).

In a first step to assure consumer acceptance of their Videotext/ Teletext program, the French have provided free alphanumeric terminals to replace the standard paper telephone directories (Fig. 1-13). The terminal for the electronic directory is not only compatible with standard Videotext technology, but can also be used to request information that will appear on the TV screen.

16

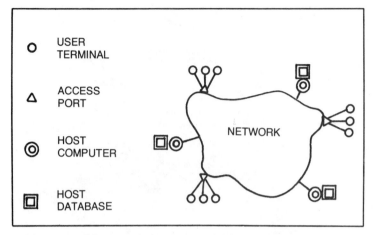

Fig. 1-12. *Telematique* public network handles all switching and network management but not data-base control.

The French program involves two services based on a common standard: Antiope is a direct one-way broadcast of radio signals through the radio network; the user selects required data for display on the screen, using the numeric keys on the terminal keyboard (Fig. 1-14). Teletel is connected directly to information stored in data bases through the telephone network. It creates an interactive dialogue with the data-processing centers. An Alphanumeric keyboard is used. (See Fig. 1-15.)

Fig. 1-13. Alphanumeric terminal used to replace standard telephone directories in French Videotext program.

Fig. 1-14. Antiope Teletext program in French *telematique*.

The French offer two equipment configurations: a unit with a decoder and alphanumeric keyboard (Fig. 1-16) and a separate modem (Fig. 1-17), and a stand-alone terminal with an integrated decoder/modem and alphanumeric keyboard (Fig. 1-18). Another product in the *telematique* program is a low-cost consumer facsimile transceiver that permits transmission of a page of paper through the existing telephone network. (See Fig. 1-19.) This equipment can also operate as a simple photocopier. And to

Fig. 1-15. French Teletel Videotext two-way home-information program.

18

Fig. 1-16. Terminal with keyboard in *telematique* program.

further expand the capabilities of the home user, telematique has also made available printers (Figs. 1-20 and 1-21)—devices that let the user save hard copy of data assembled.

The *telematique* program aims to bring computer and telecommunications technology within the reach of every Frenchman who owns a telephone. Therefore, there's another important product associated with this program—a telewriter, which permits the simultaneous transmission of

Fig. 1-17. Separate modem in the *telematique* program.

Fig. 1-18. Stand-alone terminal with integrated modem used in *telematique* program.

written material. (See Fig. 1-22.) Using multiplexing techniques, the input from a pressure-sensitive graphic tablet (either manuscript or sketches) is conveyed in the segment of speech bandwidth—that is, between 1550 and 1950 Hz (hertz). Both ends are identically equipped with a modified TV screen, to display local copy as well as received copy. Both ends present the

Fig. 1-19. Consumer facsimile transceiver used in *telematique* program.

Fig. 1-20. One hard-copy printer used in *telematique* program.

same image to each user, and both users can write or amend simultaneously. A range of eight colors is available.

Coordinating all their efforts in bringing telecommunications to the public, the French have developed yet another program: electronic banking. In this system, a magnetic card with a built-in computer (called a *microprocessor*) can be inserted into a terminal to complete the transaction. The card has the ability to store data as well as to identify the user. It can be used

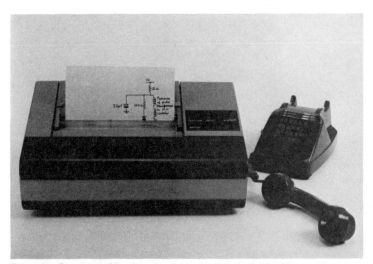

Fig. 1-21. One-type of hard-copy printer used in the *telematique* program.

21

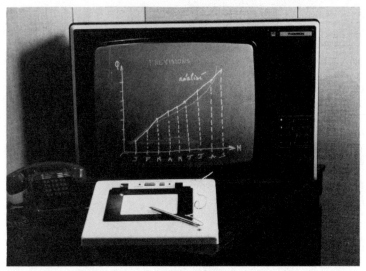

Fig. 1-22. Telewriter used in *telematique* program.

either at the point of the transaction or in home banking, providing the owner with an electronic checkbook. In home banking, the user has a terminal and a card reader (Fig. 1-23); at the point of the transaction, there's a trader terminal and the customer box for inserting his card (Fig. 1-23).

There's no way that the card can be tampered with, since it's protected by the user's code as well as the bank code. And, if three false codes are

Fig. 1-23. Electronic banking at home is possible using this terminal and special card reader to perform the transactions.

entered consecutively, the electronic elements of the card will self-destruct.

A purchase-payment transaction is performed as follows:

1. The trader inserts his pay card in his special terminal.

2. The trader keys the amount he will pay. The sum is displayed on the terminal and the customer box at the same time.

3. The customer keys his confidential code.

4. The message is generated and transmitted to the central unit, which authenticates the customer and performs the operation of validation.

5. Sums are transferred and the display announces Transaction Accepted.

6. A receipt is produced.

The operation of the electronic payment system is in five main steps (see Fig. 1-25):

1. Card customization. (This is the responsibility of the issuing bank.)

2. Initializing the card—recording of the amount of credit agreed to by the bank; and issuing the secret code.

3. Execution of payment transactions, by one of two techniques: In the *off-line mode* (guaranteed local payment), the amount paid is recorded simultaneously as a debit against the card holder and as a credit in the memory of the point of sale terminal. A ticket is then printed out.

In the *on-line mode* (guaranteed remote payment), inserting the card into the terminal connects the terminal to the computer system at the bank. After making sure that the card holder is solvent, the guarantee of payment returned to the terminal authorizes execution of the operation.

Fig. 1-24. Electronic banking at the point of transaction uses a special card reader (left) and special terminal (center). The latter connects to the customer's card reader for proper interaction.

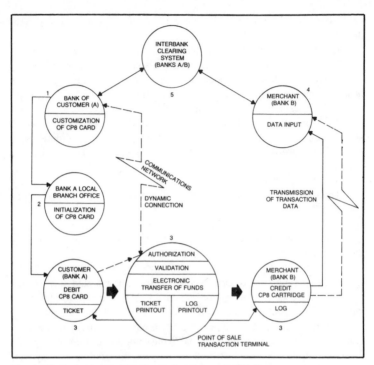

Fig. 1-25. System operation in electronic banking/trading.

4. Transmission of data to the computer system at the bank where the card holder has his or her account.

5. Updating of accounts affected by the transaction—automatic, computerized updating of customer's account.

SUMMARY

The *telematique* system in particular is an excellent first try at providing universal digital services to an entire population. Such a system combined with American knowhow could well become a world standard. In any event, every new home-information development helps to acquaint and familiarize the general public with the various aspects of home computerism.

But home computers can do much more than any individual system can, at least at present. They can optimize your energy use; monitor your doors and windows to provide a security system; and perform such information storage and retrieval tasks as recording your medical records, car maintenance history, tax information, and insurance records.

Indeed, the home computer is a far more powerful and flexible device than any overall system presently available. In the next chapter you'll see what exactly makes that computer "tick."

Chapter 2

What Is a Computer?

```
•  30124 75152 42061
   JACK PALMER
            31-12-81
```

What exactly is a home computer? Well, to come up with an answer we may as well begin at the beginning by asking what a computer is—ignoring the "home" distinction for the moment.

A "counting, calculating device" is a simple but sound definition. Taking a look at the verb, to "compute," according to *Webster's*, is "to determine or calculate (by means of a computer)."

One thing we do know for sure: computers have been around for quite a while. The 5,000-year-old abacus is a mechanical calculating aid, and as such fits our definition, certainly. In comparatively modern times, Leonardo da Vinci described in his drawings a machine that would maintain a constant ratio of 10:1 in each of its 13-digit registering wheels.

In the seventeenth century, John Napier, the discoverer of the logarithm, developed a movable multiplication table mode of bone strips on which numbers had been stamped. Somewhat later, the French philosopher and mathematician Blaise Pascal put together a machine that could add and subtract using precisely interconnected gears. It included a ratchet device that communicated, by one revolution of one wheel, a movement of one digit to the wheel of the next highest order.

Other important milestones along the path to computers as we know them today are: the Charles Babbage analytical machine, which included instructions on punched cards and a memory element where numbers were stored; the Billings and Hollerith electrical tabulating machine; and—the great breakthroughs—the isolation of radio waves and the development of the cathode-ray tube (CRT), vacuum tube, and transistor.

The first electronic computers were developed between 1932 and the late '50s. Between 1960 and 1965, highly sophisticated transistorized computers entered the marketplace, after which the development of computers increased by leaps and bounds. The introduction of the microprocessor in 1971 is considered to be the most important invention of this period.

COMPUTERS AND INTELLIGENCE

The above is a ridiculously short synopsis of the history of computers. (Many good books are available on the subject; by all means, get one!) Still, it may serve our purposes. One really important thing to keep in mind is that computers literally don't have the brains of a mosquito. No computer can think. It can, however, be set—or *programmed*—to do certain simple-minded tasks very quickly. So, it's fairly easy for intelligent humans to write programs that make the computer *seem* intelligent.

Just as computers have no real intelligence, though, neither are they capable of compassion or malice. When computers seem helpful and considerate, it's only because their programs were written that way by living, breathing humans. And that malice computers sometimes seem to show is usually attributable to the shortcomings of the programs written by those same humans.

If you feel at all "anxious" in working with computers, it has nothing to do with the machines themselves. Perhaps it has something to do with your feeling of "loss of control," but—to be fair—any ill will such a loss engenders should be directed to the humans controlling the machines, rather than to the computers directly. After all, you can't blame the computers for such "Big Brother" aspirations as the massive computer systems operated by the IRS and various other government organizations. The computers aren't gnashing their teeth to audit you: they only follow the instructions given them by Government people.

Now that we've seen what a computer can't do (think) and what it can do (follow orders), let's see what it's made of.

BASIC COMPUTER COMPONENTS

Computers consist of four parts: central processing unit, memory, input/output circuitry, and peripheral units.

Central Processing Unit (CPU). This is the element that performs all arithmetic calculations, makes all logical decisions, controls access to the computer by input and output devices, stores and retrieves data from the memory, and coordinates the orderly execution of the program. The heart of the CPU is the microprocessor.

Memory. Memory is the element that holds ("remembers") data entered into it. To be useful, the CPU (the "brain" of the computer) must be coupled with some sort of memory; otherwise, the CPU will only execute functions, without placing them in memory for storage until needed for later use.

Input/Output (I/O) Circuitry. This provides the computer's connection to external devices. Without such circuitry, the CPU and memory would continue to interact with each other, but without sharing the

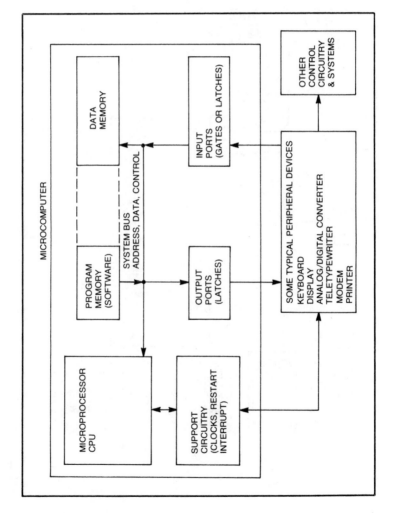

Fig. 2-1. Typical block diagram of computer system.

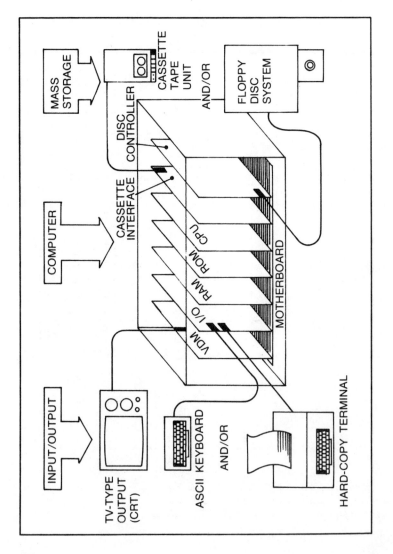

Fig. 2-2. Three-dimensional view of computer system.

benefit of that interaction with the outside world. I/O circuitry connects to devices that show us the performed interactions—that show us "what's happening in there."

Peripheral Units. These devices are needed to "read" (or to ascertain) what the CPU and memory have been up to, and to "write" (transmit) to these two components what we want them to know.

Figure 2-1 shows a block diagram of a typical computer and its components; Fig. 2-2 illustrates the physical appearance of these components.

Peripheral units can be subdivided in two categories: additional memory storage (discussed in Chapter 3) and communication I/O devices (discussed shortly). Of course, when we say "communicate," the next logical question is: How do I/O devices communicate? That, too, will be discussed shortly.

MICROPROCESSOR

The microprocessor is an example of what's called a large-scale integrated circuit, or LSI. Don't be mislead by the term "large," though: the device would fit easily on your fingernail, with room to spare.

The microprocessor consists of an accumulator, arithmetic logic unit, read-write memory, register, decoder for instructions, program counter and address register stack, timing and control section, parallel data and I/O bus, and controller for input and output data. The read-write memory, being part of the microprocessor (which is in turn part of the CPU), should not be confused with the memory mentioned earlier, which is external to the CPU.

All microprocessors work using the binary numbers 0 or 1. Just as a light switch on the wall in your room is either on or off, the solid-state switches inside a microprocessor have only two states of operation. "On" means that current is conducted, while "off" means that current is stopped. *This single, one-piece on/off switching operation is the basis of all complex computer programming and design.*

Transistors

The switching itself is accomplished by a variety of components in a number of ways. The basic component is the *transistor*—a device for controlling current between two terminals. The transistor has two important functions in solid-state electronic circuits: to provide gain or amplification of the electric current and to facilitate electronic switching (Fig. 2-3).

There are two different modes of switching: bipolar and unipolar. *Bipolar* switching (Fig. 2-4) refers to the action in those transistors in which the working current flows through two types of *semiconductor* material, called N-type and P-type. (A semiconductor is a substance whose electric conductivity is intermediate between that of a metal and an insulator.) Here, the working current consists of both positive and negative electrical charges. Such bipolar transistors operate faster than unipolar transistors, but they take up more space on a chip and cost more to manufacture.

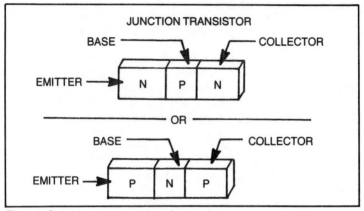

Fig. 2-3. Switching characteristics of a transistor.

In unipolar transistors (Fig. 2-5), the working current flows through only one type of semiconductor material, either N-type or P-type. In this case, the working current consists of either positive or negative electrical charges, but never both. All MOS transistors are unipolar. (MOS stands for metal oxide semiconductor—a semiconductor manufacturing technology used to produce integrated circuit logic components.)

The MOS transistors most widely used in integrated circuits are MOSFETs—metal oxide semiconductor field-effect transistors. (See Fig. 2-6.) These transistors are very small and can be manufactured in a few simple steps.

Diodes

Another component widely used in microprocessor operation is the *diode*—a device that exhibits a high resistance when a voltage is applied in one direction and a low resistance when a voltage is applied in the other direction. This is achieved with semiconductors, fabricating a junction of N and P material. The characteristics of this junction are such that current flows more rapidly in one direction than in the other (Fig. 2-7).

Let's examine some other components and functions of the microprocessor.

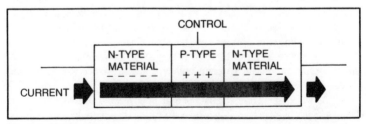

Fig. 2-4. Bipolar transistor.

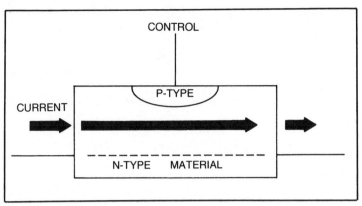

Fig. 2-5. Unipolar transistor.

Accumulator. This includes a register and its related circuitry that hold an operand for arithmetic and logic operations.

Register. A fast-access circuit used to store the 0s and 1s (bits), we'll learn more about it later on.

Arithmetic Logic Unit (ALU). This is the part of the CPU that executes adds, subtracts, shifts, and logic operations.

Read-Write Memory. The contents of this memory can be continuously changed, quickly and easily, during system operation.

Program Counter. One specific register in the CPU that specifies the address of the next instruction to be fetched and executed. Normally, the program counter is incremented automatically each time an instruction is fetched.

From the descriptions above, you can see that inside the microprocessor is a register that temporarily stores the language input, and in so doing acts as a program counter. After storing the program in memory, the program counter, is set to the beginning address—or location—of the program. When you execute the microprocessor's action, the program counter addresses the first memory location; the memory responds by feeding the first instruction to the microprocessor. After the microproces-

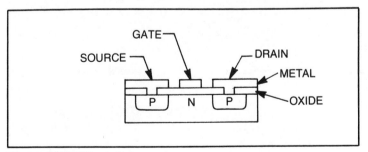

Fig. 2-6. MOSFET transistor.

sor executes the instruction, the program counter is incremented by one, and addresses the next memory location, and so on.

If you examine (Fig. 2-1) again, you'll notice that the CPU has some support circuitry. The *clock*, for example, is an electronic circuit that generates timing pulses which synchronize the operation of the computer. The *interrupt circuit* can send a signal to the computer telling it to temporarily suspend the normal sequence of a routine, and transfer control to a special routine. (Operation can be resumed from this point later on.)

The *system bus* is a group of wires that allows memory, CPU, and I/O devices (through the input and output ports) to communicate.

MEMORY

Within the confines of the computer are two memory systems—data memory and program memory. They're known under different names, however, as we shall see.

Read-Only Memory

Data memory is also called *resident memory* or *permanent memory*. Physically supplied as a module, it's the operating system or read-only memory (ROM) module. The ROM module has a program—a set of instructions that tells the computer how it is to respond to messages from the outside world. Remember, the ROM and its program are part of the computer itself.

Programs stored in ROM are called *firmware*. The data is entered by the manufacturer: it cannot be altered by the user, but neither will it be lost if power is turned off. Such operating systems are complex; however, they're essential, since they help the computer to interpret our instructions accurately. We could say that the operating system is a set of programs automates the management of all facets within the computer system; it is in

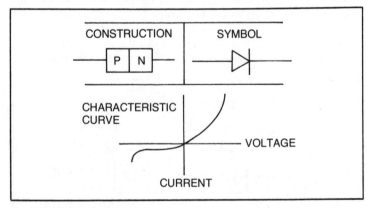

Fig. 2-7. Typical diode.

the operating system, for example, that the BASIC language resides—the language used by most personal/home computers, described in Chapter 5.

For hobbyists who want to write their own operating systems there are ROM memories available that can be altered or erased. These are referred to as programmable read-only memory or PROM, which means that the programmer can program this memory—*but only once*: once a PROM has been programmed, it becomes a ROM and cannot be altered further.

Erasable PROMs (EPROMs) can be programmed and erased and thus reprogrammed. Erasing is accomplished by directing a strong ultraviolet light through a small quartz window in the chip. The more recently developed electrically alterable ROM (EAROM) uses electrical signals to erase the ROM contents.

Random-Access Memory

The program memory—the second memory in the computer—is the random-access memory or RAM. It's also called temporary memory and read-write memory. Using your input and output devices, you can store memory in and retrieve memory from RAM. However, if electrical power should be cut off, the memory is not retained in RAM.

Both RAM and ROM memories are contained on so-called memory boards or modules. These boards have a number of silicon chips. Each chip contains thousands of individual storage cells, or *bits*. (A bit is the smallest unit of information a computer deals with.)

These cells are organized in a variety of ways—for example, a 1,024-bit memory can be structured as a 1,024-×-1-bit word, or as a 256-×-4-bit words. Each bit is either an On or an Off in an electrical circuit; that is, it's a two-value system—a bit can have a value of either zero or one. (A *word* is the number of bits needed to represent a computer instruction, to the number of bits needed to represent the largest data element normally processed by a computer. The second number tells you how much memory the computer can use at one time. Most personal/home computers are xxxx-×-8-bit-word.

Memory is measured in thousands (K) of bytes, each byte is equal to 8 bits. The amount of memory a computer contains is described in various ways. In the Apple II computer, for example, the 6502 single-board computer memory is capable of holding up to 48K *bytes* of programmable memory (RAM). Up to 16K bytes of ROM space are also available.

Inside the console of the Atari computer are the CPU and the memory bank containing the operating system's 10K ROM module plus 8K bytes of RAM. That means that with the basic Atari 800 computer, you can randomly put in, change if necessary, and receive at any time 8,000 bytes (or 64,000 bits) of information. You also have available 10,000 bytes (80,000 bits) of information that can neither be erased nor reprogrammed. This potential of 10K ROM remains dormant until you add the software.

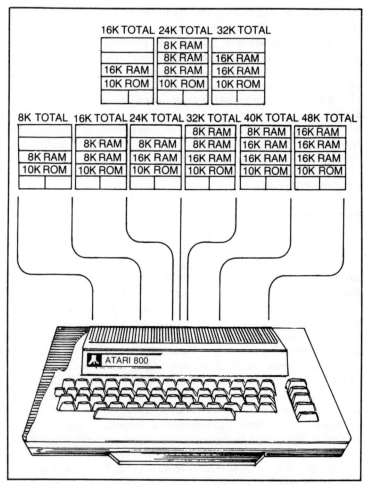

16K TOTAL	24K TOTAL	32K TOTAL
	8K RAM	
	8K RAM	16K RAM
16K RAM	8K RAM	16K RAM
10K ROM	10K ROM	10K ROM

8K TOTAL	16K TOTAL	24K TOTAL	32K TOTAL	40K TOTAL	48K TOTAL
			8K RAM	8K RAM	16K RAM
	8K RAM	8K RAM	8K RAM	16K RAM	16K RAM
8K RAM	8K RAM	16K RAM	16K RAM	16K RAM	16K RAM
10K ROM	10K ROM	10K ROM	10K ROM	10K ROM	10K ROM

Fig. 2-8. Adding additional memory to the Atari 800 computer.

Many personal/home computers are designed to accommodate additional memory (Fig. 2-8). The Atari 800 computer manual instructs you as follows:

> This module contains approximately 8,000 storage cells for your computer to use. You may want to expand the capacity of your computer system to allow you to use and write longer programs. Expansion is accomplished by inserting additional RAM memory modules into the empty sockets of the memory bank. These modules are available in 8K and 16K versions. Inside the memory bank you'll see four module sockets, two of which are already occupied with the Operating System 10K ROM and one 8K RAM module. The Operat-

ing System 10K ROM must remain in the front socket. The other three sockets are available for expanding your computer's RAM memory in a variety of combinations.

COMMUNICATIONS

We're all familiar with the telephone as a medium of communication. The analog signal that mirrors our human voice by modifying an electric current along a transmission path is the predominant transmission method in the world's telephone networks. While the analog technique transmits speech patterns both faithfully and economically, it is not designed to handle the rapid transmission of large amounts of information. Restrictions are inherent in the extremely limited bandwidth of voice channels.

As we have seen, the computer is a much faster medium of communicating—although we've seen too that the computer is basically a switching system, functioning much as a telephone network as it routes traffic through a series of switches in a controlled and orderly fashion. A computer uses its stream of on/off pulses to send data in digital form along a transmission path at very high speeds.

When you speak over the telephone, your voice creates an analog waveform: that is, in terms of its highs and lows and degrees of strength, the wave is analogous to your own voice. It is not broken into discrete bits, as in digital transmission. Your speech enters a transmission channel, passes through the telephone company's office and switching equipment, and arrives at its destination.

Transmission frequencies are described in terms of hertz (Hz), rather than cycles per second (cps). Normal sound will vary from 30 to 20,000 Hz. An analog signal, like your voice, would look like a wave in a diagram. The wave constantly changes its height and breadth.

The digital transmission stream consists of on/off pulses called *bits*. A bit represents the choice between the zero or one—or mark or space, to use the language computers talk. Bits take up much less space in transmission, so the channel can be packed with much more conversation or data. Digital and analog transmission can't be mixed together: digital language must first be converted to analog language in order to travel over an analog circuit, and vice versa. These conversions are made by modems, which we'll discuss later the book.

BINARY SYSTEM

When something can exist in only one of two states at any given time, there can be no ambiguity: it's either on or it's off. Let's take a row of lights as an example. Since each light represents two states (and only two)—on and off—it can also represent two numbers. If it's off, it stands for zero; if it's on, its value is determined by the digit one.

Binary-Coded Decimals

The binary-coded decimal (BCD) uses four binary digits to represent

Table 2-1. Binary-Coded Decimals

Switch Position	Lamp Number / Binary Code				OP: 0=zero
	4(2^3=8)	3(2^2=4)	2(2^1=2)	1(2^0=1)	
Off (0)	0	0	0	0	
On (1)	8	4	2	1	

the decimal numbers 0 through 9. The BCD is a weighted code wherein each bit has a weight that is an integer power of 2: e.g., 2^3=8; 2^2=4; 2^1=2; 2^0=1. (Remember that any number raised to the zero power equals 1.)

Using the lights again as an example, let's say we have four lamps set up and designated as follows: 8 4 2 1. To show a 1, we light up lamp 1; 3 is represented by lighting up both lamps 2 and 1. (See Table 2-1.)

The 4-bit binary code 1011 (that is, on-off-on-on) can easily be translated into a decimal number using Table 2-1:

Off   0   0   0   0
On   8   4   2   1

This means that 1011 = [8-on] + [4-off] + [2-on] + [1-on] = 8 + 0 + 2 + 1 = 11 decimal.

Octal and Hexadecimal

In the 4-bit binary system shown above, only the numbers 0 through 15 (a total of 16 numbers) can be represented, as shown in Table 2-2. But by using more bits, each having a weight which is the next higher power of 2, we can represent as large a number as we wish, still using the binary code. Since three bits can be used to represent eight numbers (0 through 7), and four bits to represent sixteen numbers, there's a convenient method of grouping these bits three or four at a time, connecting each group. This is done by the use of codes called *octal* and *hexadecimal*. These codes are more compact and much easier to use than long strings of binary 1's and 0's.

Looking at Table 2-3, you'll note that a long 4-bit binary number is represented by a single octal digit (or two, depending upon the string of bits). The hexadecimal system, also called "destination hex," is the most popular numbering system in computing. Most computers use 8-bit bytes—another way of saying that, generally speaking, a byte is a string of 8 bits. Because of the nature of computer storage systems and procedures, a byte is the amount of storage space needed to represent a character, numeral, letter, symbol, or blank. A kilobyte is 1,000 bytes (or 8,000 bits) and a megabyte is 1 million bytes (or 8 million bits, or one-half million 16-bit *words*). A word is the number of bits needed to represent a computer instruction, or the number of bits needed to represent the largest data element normally processed by a computer. One hexadecimal character can represent a 4-bit "nibble"; two hex characters an 8-bit byte; and four hex characters, a 16-bit word.

The hexadecimal system is therefore more convenient, since it represents a more readable representation of internal data than an arrangement of binary bits and digits. As you can see from Table 2-3, it takes only 2 digits selected from the numeric character set 0-9 and the six letters A-F to represent a byte (8 bits) of information, as opposed to the eight digits needed to represent the same number in an external binary form.

Let's take a look now at Table 2-4, the octal number system. The base for this system is 8. To determine the decimal number from the octal number 5763, say, we'd follow these steps:

$$5763 = 5000 = 2560 \text{ (octal code 5 in the 4-digit row)}$$
$$763 = 448 \text{ (octal code 7 in the 3-digit row)}$$
$$63 = 48 \text{ (octal code 6 in the 2-digit row)}$$
$$3 = \underline{3} \text{ (octal code 3 in the 1-digit row)}$$
$$3059 \text{ decimal}$$

Table 2-5 shows the hexadecimal number system. Similarly to octal, when we want to transfer the hexadecimal number into a decimal number we do so as follows:

$$3CB6 = 3 = 12288 \text{ (hex code 3 in column 4)}$$
$$C = 3072 \text{ (hex code C in column 3)}$$
$$B = 176 \text{ (hex code B in column 2)}$$
$$6 = \underline{6} \text{ (hex code 6 in column 1)}$$
$$15542 \text{ decimal.}$$

Before characters such as punctuation marks and other special symbols can be processed by computers, they must first be changed to 0's and 1's. The most common code for accomplishing this is the ASCII—American Standard Code for Information Exchange. The code uses a definition 256 different standard meanings for the 8-bit code. This easily accommodates all letters, in both upper- and lowercase, punctuation marks, symbols, and so forth.

Table 2-2. 4-Bit Binary System

Decimal	BCD		8 4 2 1
0	0000	=	off-off-off-off
1	0001	=	off-off-off-on
2	0010	=	off-off-on-off
3	0011	=	off-off-on-on
4	0100	=	off-on-off-off
5	0101	=	off-on-off-on
6	0110	=	off-on-on-off
7	0111	=	off-on-on-on
8	1000	=	on-off-off-off
9	1001	=	on-off-off-on
10	1010	=	on-off-on-off
11	1011	=	on-off-on-on
12	1100	=	on-on-off-off
13	1101	=	on-on-off-on
14	1110	=	on-on-on-off
15	1111	=	on-on-on-on

Table 2-3. Comparison of Numbering Systems

Binary	Decimal	Octal	Hexadecimal
0000	0	00	0
0001	1	01	1
0010	2	02	2
0011	3	03	3
0100	4	04	4
0101	5	05	5
0110	6	06	6
0111	7	07	7
1000	8	10	8
1001	9	11	9
1010	10	12	A
1011	11	13	B
1100	12	14	C
1101	13	15	D
1110	14	16	E
1111	15	17	F

While it isn't necessary that you, as a home-computer user, know how to do hex arithmetic, it could be helpful to understand the relationship between hex and decimal values. To assist you in finding these relationships, we've provided Table 2-6—a conversion table for hex to decimal (and vice versa). To use this table, simply follow the right- or left-hand column down until you find the first hex digit—that is, the high-order digit—in your number. Then follow the row across until you come to the intersection with the second hex digit (the low-order digit). The number in the square is the decimal equivalent of the hex value you're looking up.

Similarly, when you know the decimal value and want to convert to hex, find the decimal value in the Table, and follow the column up to the top

Table 2-4. Octal Number System

Octal Code	4	3	2	1
	$(8^3=512)$	$(8^2=64)$	$(8^1=8)$	$(8^0=1)$
0	0	0	0	0
1	512	64	8	1
2	1024	128	16	2
3	1536	192	24	3
4	2048	256	32	4
5	2560	320	40	5
6	3072	384	48	6
7	3584	448	56	7

Table 2-5. Hexadecimal Number System

Hexadecimal Code	4 ($16^3=4096$)	3 ($16^2=256$)	2 ($16^1=16$)	1 ($16^0=1$)
0	0	0	0	0
1	4096	256	16	1
2	8192	512	32	2
3	12288	768	48	3
4	16384	1024	64	4
5	20480	1280	80	5
6	24576	1536	96	6
7	28672	1792	112	7
8	32768	2048	128	8
9	36864	2304	144	9
A	40960	2560	160	10
B	45056	2816	176	11
C	49152	3072	192	12
D	53248	3328	208	13
E	57344	3584	224	14
F	61440	3840	240	15

to find the rightmost, low-order digit. Then follow the row to the right or left to find the leftmost, high-order digit. For example, decimal 179 is hex B3.

COMPUTER LANGUAGES

Computers, like humans, communicate in a definite "language."

Machine Language

The lowest form of computer language is *machine language*, which uses the binary numbers discussed above. As we've seen, this binary system is cumbersome, prone to errors, and very time-consuming. We've also seen that we can easily replace binary language with octal or hexadecimal numbers. Yet even octal or hex codes can be difficult to learn and to

Table 2-6. Hexadecimal Conversion Chart

Second Hex Digit

First Hex Digit	0	1	2	3	4	5	6	7	8	9	A	B	C	D	E	F
0	0	1	2	3	4	5	6	7	8	9	10	11	12	13	14	15
1	16	17	18	19	20	21	22	23	24	25	26	27	28	29	30	31
2	32	33	34	35	36	37	38	39	40	41	42	43	44	45	46	47
3	48	49	50	51	52	53	54	55	56	57	58	59	60	61	62	63
4	64	65	66	67	68	69	70	71	72	73	74	75	76	77	78	79
5	80	81	82	83	84	85	86	87	88	89	90	91	92	93	94	95
6	96	97	98	99	100	101	102	103	104	105	106	107	108	109	110	111
7	112	113	114	115	116	117	118	119	120	121	122	123	124	125	126	127
8	128	129	130	131	132	133	134	135	136	137	138	139	140	141	142	143
9	144	145	146	147	148	149	150	151	152	153	154	155	156	157	158	159
A	160	161	162	163	164	165	166	167	168	169	170	171	172	173	174	175
B	176	177	178	179	180	181	182	183	184	185	186	187	188	189	190	191
C	192	193	194	195	196	197	198	199	200	201	202	203	204	205	206	207
D	208	209	210	211	212	213	214	215	216	217	218	219	220	221	222	223
E	224	225	226	227	228	229	230	231	232	233	234	235	236	237	238	239
F	240	241	242	243	244	245	246	247	248	249	250	251	252	253	254	255

remember. In any event, machine-language programming is useful only to those who want to learn programming skills or to use the computer for teaching computer operation.

Assembly Language

Because machine language is difficult another language has been developed: assembly language. In assembly language, the numbers that represent commands in machine language are replaced by shorthand expressions for computer instructions, addresses, and data. These instructions are referred to as *mnemonics*—instructions that are easy to remember. (The word *mnemonics* comes from the Greek word for memory.) For example, LDA = load accumulator register in mnemonics. Mnemonics are used in place of binary, octal, or hex code when writing a program.

Although mnemonics certainly make programming easier, the computer still understands only one language: the on/off of the binary code, or machine language. Therefore, we have to translate our assembly language into machine language before the computer can understand it. For instance, we have to translate the mnemonic STOR A—Store the item A—into some combination of 1s and 0s. The translation is done with an *assembler*—a program loaded into the computer's memory by the manufacturer.

When programming in assembly language, we talk in terms of the *source program*. (You are the *source* of the *program*.) This source program is the input to the assembler, which performs the translation into 1s and 0s and generates the appropriate machine code. The resultant machine program is called the *object code*—the actual binary machine instructions and data the computer can understand and use.

However, as with machine language, assembly language, too, has a number of disadvantages.First of all, it's machine-dependent, meaning that given assembly-language program can rarely be run on any model of computer other than the one it was written for. Thus, each program must be rewritten for each new model computer on which it is to be run. Another disadvantage is that the user still finds this language no easier to use than machine language.

High-Level Languages

To bridge these gaps, computer designers have come up with what are called *high-level languages*. The earliest of these languages were developed to meet specific needs. COBOL, or Common Business Oriented Language, was developed to meet the needs of business, and FORTRAN, or Formula Translator, specifically for mathematical calculations.

High-level languages use English in their statement structure and syntax. They are, therefore, easier for an English-speaking user to learn. Also, these languages are machine-independent: a program written in FORTRAN can be run with little or no modification on any computer for which a FORTRAN program is available.

Although high-level languages are easy for you to understand and use, they are not understood by the computer, which "speaks" only in machine language. They must therefore be translated into machine language, and this is done with either a *compiler* or an *interpreter*, computer programs (software) that translate or decode each high-level code or instruction into a machine code or instruction.

There is one major difference between compilers and interpreters. An interpreter stays in memory with the text and executes the text as it decodes it. It must decode the text everytime it runs the program. A compiler decodes all text first and then erases itself from memory. The decoded program can be executed directly by the computer without further decoding. This means that a program translated or "compiled" by a compiler runs much faster and can be much longer than an "interpreted" program because nothing else is sharing memory space with it.

BASIC

The language used in almost all home/personal computers is BASIC (for Beginners All-purpose Symbolic Instruction Code). It can be learned in several days by a noncomputer-oriented layman.

Virtually all versions of BASIC designed for personal/home computers use interpreters—in contrast with most other high-level languages, which use compilers—to process data into machine language.

When you order a computer, it already has a built-in BASIC interpreter; you simply turn it on, and it's ready for immediate use. The marvelous aspect of this is that you cannot make a permanent error when programming, because the interpreter in the computer lets you know as soon as you do so. Other languages inform you of your mistakes at the end of the program, when you're ready to start running it; BASIC makes you stop at each step when and where you make an error.

The easy-to-use and easy-to-learn aspects of BASIC go hand in hand: BASIC is a simple-minded subset of technician's English. Most of the commands are English words, and conversational statements and free-style input are permitted. Just as important is BASIC's easy and safe program modification. Each line begins with a number that specifies the order in which the statements are to be performed. Since the computer sorts out the program before running it, your statements don't have to be put into any specific order.

BASIC comes in a number of different versions, depending upon the computer manufacturer. However, because these versions do not conform to the National Standard Institute, most programs in one BASIC can be run using another BASIC of equal or greater complexity, with few or no modifications. The interpreter is what makes BASIC so easy to use. Before looking at how this works, though, let's go back a few steps and take a second look at some of the terminology used.

As you know, the programs that a computer uses are referred to as software. Software is the intelligent complement of the hardware (the CPU, peripherals, etc.), since it tells the computer what to do. There are two types of software—*systems software* and *applications software.* Systems software includes all the programs and languages built into the computer. It's the software you apply when you want to develop your own applications software.

Applications software is, as the name implies, a program you apply to certain specific functions or applications. In most cases, you'll buy applications software in the form of ready-to-use floppy discs or cassette tapes. These may include such things as games, checkbook-balancing or appliance-control setups, or whatever.

The software side of computers has always been somewhat confusing. The important thing for you to remember is that, when you get your personal/home computer, *its operating system is in the BASIC language.* This means that BASIC is permanently stored in ROM. You'll interact with your computer through the operating system (OS): the OS fields all your requests for services and manages all the resources of the computer system.

Going back to the interpreter, this program also stays in memory, where it interprets and executes the BASIC source program. It's the interaction between the OS and the BASIC interpreter that makes the personal/home computer "interactive."

To discuss BASIC in detail would be beyond the scope of this book, especially since a massive amount of literature on the subject is available. We will, however, come back to it when we discuss various peripherals.

Many of the following terms have already been defined for you (or are defined in the Glossary), but it may help to review them here. They're key terms you'll use again and again as a home-computer user.

Applications software—Programs or groups of programs that perform specific functions, such as checkbook-balancing and home-security monitoring.

BASIC—Simplified program language widely used in personal/home computers.

Compiler—A program that translates the high-level language statements of a program into machine-readable form.

Custom software—Programs designed to fit the specific needs of the user.

High-level language—Programming language containing English statements that the compiler or interpreter translates into machine language.

Interactive software—Programs that ask questions of the user and act on his responses.

Interpreter—A program that translates each statement of a high-level language into machine language as each is entered on the keyboard. An interpreter is generally used with BASIC.

Machine language—A language consisting of strings of 1s and 0s that the computer understands directly.

Operating system—A series of programs, generally provided by the manufacturer as part of the computer system, that controls such physical operations of the computer as printing and accepting input from the keyboard.

Packaged software—Off-the-shelf software.

Program—A set of coded instructions directing a computer to perform a particular function.

Programming language—A set of words and rules that constitutes a language understood by computer and user alike.

Software—A general term for computer programs.

Systems software—Those programs—interpreters and operating systems—that coordinate the operations of the various elements of a computer system.

Utility programs—Software that performs such frequently required processes as sorting, deleting, and copying.

Chapter 3
Peripheral,
or Mass, Storage

CP8

30124 75152 42061

JACK PALMER

31-12-81

The devices that are used for external, mass-storage adjuncts of the computer, are called *peripherals* and there are several kinds, such as cassette recorder, floppy disc, and fixed-disc drive. They are the type of memory system you use with the applications programs we talked about in Chapter 2. For example, if your computer has ROM BASIC and you have a checkbook-balancing software program, you'll need a cassette recorder or some other storage device in order to use the software—in other words; in order to have the RAM program interact with the ROM in the computer.

It's necessary to use a built-in cassette *interface* device or disc controller in order to let these peripherals communicate with the computer—and of course that means it's "back to 1s and 0s again"! (An interface is a synchronization of digital data transmission between a computer and an input device.) Since a cassette recorder is an analog device, the interface is responsible for translanting the analog signals into digital patterns. On the other hand, a disc drive is a digital peripheral, so here the controller—which in fact interfaces the drive with the computer—must see to it that the right thing happens at the right time between the disc drive and the computer.

CASSETTE RECORDER

The simplest and least expensive way to store additional memory is on a regular cassette recorder. By recording data on tape, in digital form, you can keep the data as a permanent record. Later, you can load this data from the cassette recorder into the computer's memory when you want to use the information again.

You can move a program between the computer and a cassette. However, since the motor control of a cassette recorder varies from manufacturer to manufacturer, some computer suppliers recommend certain brands of recorders, or even supply their own line of recorders—the Atari Company, for one. Whatever the brand, though, cassette recorders are slow, sequential in nature, and finicky in terms of reliability.

Since the cassette recorder is such a well-known device, and since information about it is readily available in a variety of books, we won't get into its basic functions here. (Chapter 4 discusses the operations of down- and off-loading from a cassette recorder.)

FLOPPY DISC

A floppy disc operates basically like a record player. The disc (which even looks like a small phonograph record) fits on a spindle inside a drive, turning the drive around (though at a much faster speed than a record player—300 rpm versus 33⅓ rpm). Within the disc drive system, a record/playback head (called a read/write head) either reads (receives) data on the disc or writes (transmits) this data. The head—the equivalent of the record-player arm—is mounted on a positioner, which moves the head laterally across the disc to any area requested by the computer.

Like a record player, a floppy-disc drive (Figs. 3-1 and 3-2) has a motor to power its drive system.

Discs are available in single- and double-sided versions, with single density (normal) or double density data-storage capacity. The disc (Fig. 3-3) itself is a flat, circular piece of flexible Mylar plastic, coated with a metallic oxide. The plastic disc is sealed inside a square plastic jacket that is either 8

Fig. 3-1. Floppy-disc drive. (Courtesy, Parasitic Engineering, Inc.)

Fig. 3-2. Integrated-circuit board used in disc drive. (Courtesy, Parasitic Engineering, Inc.)

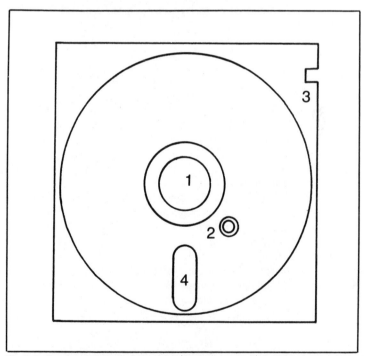

Fig. 3-3. Overhead view of a floppy disk: (1) large center hole; (2) index or, sector sensing hole; (3) square notch; (4) read/write notch.

or 5¼ inches to a side. To protect the disc from dust, fingerprints, and similar contaminants, it is never removed from the jacket: the whole package is inserted in the slot of the disc drive. When the drive is turned on, a hub—which spins the disc inside its jacket—comes up (or down) and seats itself in the large center hole.

As the disc spins around, the system senses each revolution by means of a small hole located near the large center hole of the disc. There's only one such sensing (index or sector) hole if the disc is used in a soft-sectored technique, but a number of holes if the disc is hard-sectored. (See Fig. 3-4.)

Also as the disc spins around, the sector hole passes a photo cell on each revolution of the disk. The controller determines the format of data on the tracks. In a single-density format, each track contains 26 sectors, each of which holds 128 bytes of user data. In this configuration, each surface of the disk holds 77 tracks, for a total of 256,256 bytes of data. (A double-density disk holds twice as much—512,512 bytes per surface. (See Fig. 3-5.)

Hard-sectored discs have 32 equally spaced sector holes. The sensing of a sector hole signals the start of a sector, where the number of bytes is fixed (128 bytes in single-density format, 256 in double-density). The total yield here is 315,392 and 630,784 bytes per surface, respectively. As you can see, soft-sectored discs hold more data storage than the hard-sectored ones. For this reason, and also because soft-sectored mechanisms are less complex, soft-sectored discs are more popular than the hard-sectored versions. (Incidentally, soft-sectored and hard-sectored drives are not compatible—you can't use one with the other.)

When you purchase custom software with data stored on a disc, you'll find that a tab has been placed on one side of the jacket. This tab covers up a square notch, preventing you from writing (that is, putting information) on the disc; you can only read (take information) from the disc. If you want to use a blank disc to both read and write, you have to remove the tab in order to be able to perform both functions.

The disc also has an oval opening called the read/write notch. This opening allows the read/write head of the drive to either put data on the disc or take information from it.

As mentioned before, the disc is spun by a hub assembly. The hub is driven by a drive motor that can have speeds anywhere from 300 to 3600 rpm, depending on the cost of the drive. A stepper motor controls the movement of the read/write head across the surface of the disc. Electronic circuitry controls these functions, as well as the interaction with the controller in the computer. The controller translates the computer's requests for data into physical operations that the drive has to perform in order to retrieve or store data. It is probably unnecessary to add, finally, that the floppy-disc drive system is a very delicate one and should be treated accordingly.

If you review the specifications offered by various floppy-disc manufacturers, most or all of the following will be considered:

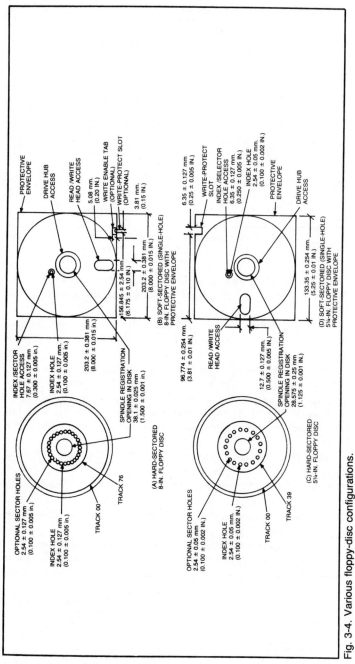

Fig. 3-4. Various floppy-disc configurations.

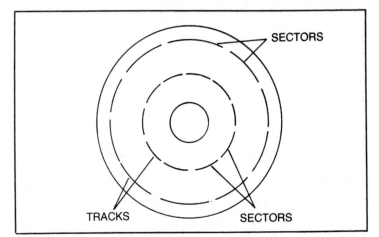

Fig. 3-5. Tracks (concentric circles) and sectors (subdivisions of each track) in a floppy disc.

Dual-or Single-Sided. On a dual-sided disc, data may be read from or written on both sides of the disc; on a single-sided disc, you can use only one side.

Double or Single Density. Density refers to bytes per track. A double-density disc will therefore hold twice as many bytes per track than a single-density disc.

Tracks. The number of tracks available with the system is usually specified. In the case of dual-sided systems, the number of tracks is the total number found by adding the number of tracks on each side of the disk.

Sectors. Sectors are subdivisions each track is divided into by the system. Bytes-per-sector indicates the number of characters each sector will hold.

Formatted Storage Capacity. This is the total number of bytes a disc can contain after it has been formatted by the system. Proper formatting—the order in which input and output are arranged—is needed to enable the system to process your data accurately and efficiently.

Soft- or Hard-Sectored. Soft-sectored discs have one hole; hard-sectored discs have 32 holes.

Access Time. The average time interval between the moment data are called for from the storage device and the instant data are delivered. It can also mean the time between the instant at which information is ready for storage and the instant at which it is actually stored.

Transfer Rate. The speed at which accessed data is moved from one device to the next.

FIXED (HARD) DISC DRIVES

Another method of upgrading your memory is through the use of a

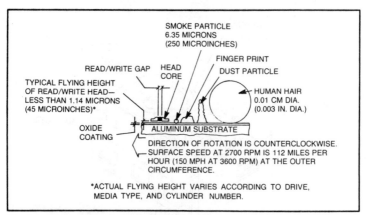

Fig. 3-6. Comparison of possible contaminations, explaining why a sealed environment is essential in a Winchester drive.

midrange Winchester disc drive, offering almost 18 megabytes of storage capacity. Even the lowest-capacity Winchester holds 5 megabytes—well over three times the data of a double-sided, double-density floppy-disc drive.

The *Winchester disc drive* shouldn't be confused with the famous rifle—although it does a bang-up job. Also known as the 3350, this *state-of-*

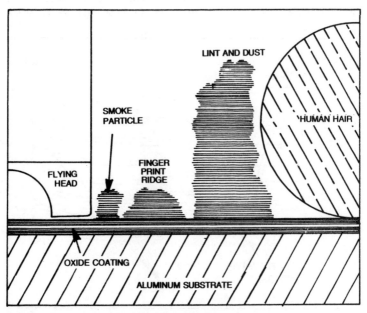

Fig. 3-7. Graphic view of a Winchester drive's sealed environment.

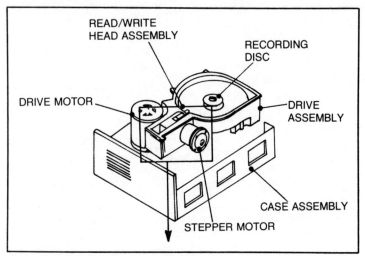

Fig. 3-8. Typical Winchester disc drive.

the-art drive incorporates nonremovable media (discs) packaged with a read/write head mechanism sealed in a module. ("State-of-the-art" means most current, or at most advanced stage of development.) The reason for storing the read/write mechanism in a sealed environment is to prevent contamination, since even a wisp of smoke, a fingerprint, a particle of dust, or a human hair could cover up or mask bits of data on the track, causing a

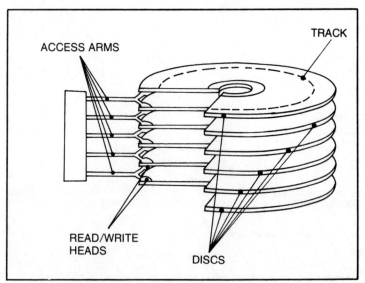

Fig. 3-9. Sealed components of Winchester disc drive.

52

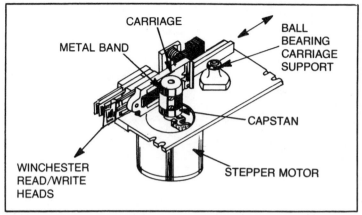

Fig. 3-10. Winchester components outside the sealed environment.

spacing loss that could result in the loss or weakening of a signal (Figs. 3-6 and 3-7). A large enough particle could even cause the read/write head to plane above it, with a resulting crash on the far side of the particle. Such a crash could easily cause serious physical damage to the disc and/or head.

There are two major families of Winchester disc storage units: 5 ¼-inch and 8-inch drives. These small Winchesters make it possible to upgrade easily from a floppy-disc drive. Also, since the average size of a Winchester unit is approximately the same as that of an 8-inch floppy-disc drive, side-by-side installation of a Winchester results in a compact configuration.

Like floppy discs the hard discs of the Winchester, have an iron oxide coating but it is on a rigid substrate, or base, of aluminum, rather than on Mylar plastic. The information on these hard discs is recorded on grooves

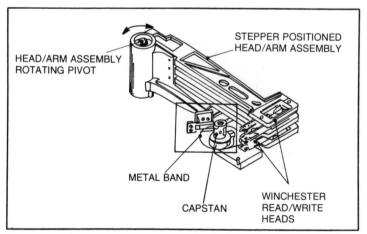

Fig. 3-11. Radial-arm position of Winchester disc drive.

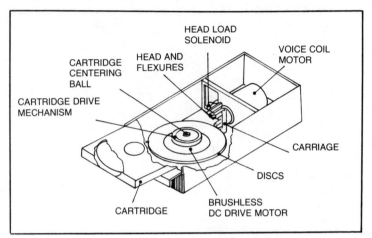

Fig. 3-12. Winchester disc drive with removable cartridge backup.

that are in concentric circles, like the rings in a tree trunk. The data contained in each such groove, or *track*, is made up of bit cells, each one a small unit of magnetic force representing one bit. Thus, a track is like a circle made up of tiny bar magnets laid end to end, each magnet being a digit in the binary number system.

Figure 3-8 shows a diagram of a typical Winchester drive. The hermetic seal wraps around the drive assembly, including the recording disc and the read/write assembly (See Fig. 3-9.) The drive motor and the head assembly stepper motor are located outside the sealed chamber (Fig. 3-10). The

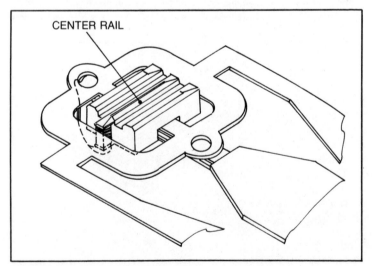

Fig. 3-13. Conventional Winchester head.

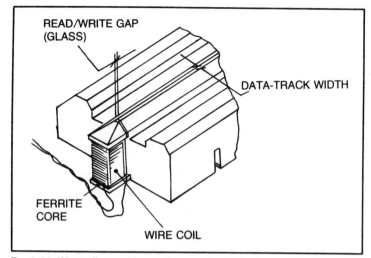

Fig. 3-14. Wire-coil-wound head of conventional Winchester drive.

stepper motor turns the capstan, upon instruction from the controller. One end of a metal band is connected to the capstan and the other end to the arm assembly. When the capstan turns, it pulls the arm to the appropriate position over the disc during read/write functions. Radial-arm positioning is shown in Fig. 3-11.

The read/write head has headpads with slots that contribute to the aerodynamic design requirement for the low-flying height of the head above the disc. The distance the head flies over the disc is 20 microns or less, which accounts for the sealed-environment requirement. With such a small distance between head and disc, it's obvious that any minute particle will cause a problem.

Another aspect to be considered in connection with the use of Winchester drives is *backup*—a means of bailing the drive out when trouble does happen. No matter how sealed the head assembly is, malfunctions can occur; and also, when a Winchester drive is completely filled with data, you have to be able to transfer this data to another medium. Here, the floppy disc comes into the picture again: any number of bytes stored on a Winchester disc can be secured by dumping the data on a like number of floppy discs. (This has to be accomplished through a manual process, however.)

The formatting and control schemes of most Winchesters and floppy-disc drives are similar enough to make mechanical and electrical interfaces between the two types a relatively simple matter. Since all Winchesters and most double-density floppy-disc drives use the modified FM (MFM) recording technique to encode and decode data, transfer from one medium to the other doesn't require special electronic circuitry.

An alternative to "media backup"—the ability to store additional data—are Winchester disc drives (called fixed drives) with a built-in fixed-

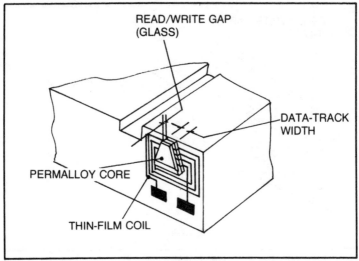

Fig. 3-15. Spiral conductors in a thin-film head.

disc/removable cartridge. Utilizing Winchester technology, these drives combine the normal sealed head, actuator, and medium (to protect from contamination) with a removable rigid-disc cartridge, typically front-loaded (Fig. 3-12).

A new technology that's becoming more and more important, since it drastically increases the storage capacity of disc drives, centers around the use of so-called *thin-film heads*. Conventional Winchester disc drive heads have a rail-like surface that confronts the disc at a distance of half a mi-

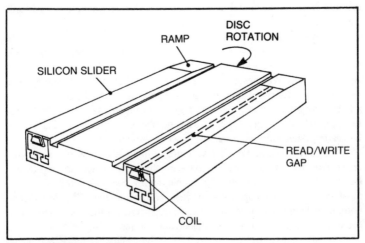

Fig. 3-16. Thin-film head.

crometer; the flow of air under the outside rails generates an aerodynamic force that supports the head. The trailing end of the center rail holds the electromagnet that reads and writes the data (Fig. 3-13). A small coil is wound around a gapped ferrite core that is attached to the end of the slider—a three-rail pad. (See Fig. 3-14.)

A thin-film head has a series of spiral conductors (Fig. 3-15), and a permalloy core, which are sputtered, or deposited, onto the outside edges of a two-rail section—a silicone substrate that becomes an integral slide. (See Fig. 3-16). Here the electromagnet also generates a supporting aerodynamic force when a disc is spinning under it.

30124 75152 42061
JACK PALMER
31-12-81

Chapter 4
Input and
Output Devices

The computer is there to receive input, process it, and relay the output back to the user. It's an incredibly dumb machine that needs you to process the information.

The most common input, of course, is the keyboard; the most common output is the video display terminal. The terminal screen is great if you only want to look at the information. If you want to retain it, you need a printer. Presently, techniques are being developed—as a matter of fact, some are already in use—to do away with the keyboard (at least for laymen's use). The thinking is that the user will be able to either touch the screen of the terminal in order to generate input, or else simply talk to the computer as if it were another human being. Both technologies are naturally quite complex in their design criteria, but both offer the utmost simplicity when it comes to "working with the computer."

THE KEYBOARD

Most keyboards available for personal/home computer use are similar in layout and "feel" to typewriter keyboards: when you press a key on the keyboard, a character is transmitted to the memory, much as to the sheet of paper in your typewriter.

Let's look at a keyboard—specifically, that of the Atari 800 computer (Figs. 4-1 and 4-2). This keyboard has alphabetic, numeric, graphic, and screen-editing functions. Each key has the capacity to be redefined by instructions from an individual cartridge; this provides you, the computer user, with the most efficient set of symbols for each application. A number of special-application cartridges and some games require that you use these key type responses or commands to the computer. Most keystrokes produce a response—a visible change—on the display screen.

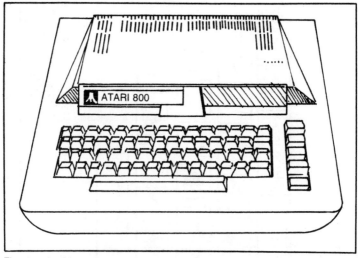

Fig. 4-1. Atari keyboard.

A glance at the keytops tells you that the keyboard closely resembles an ordinary typewriter. Pressing the CAPS/LOWR key lets you type lowercase letters, numbers, some punctuation marks, and math symbols; pressing either of the SHIFT keys will produce the uppercase letters or the character, shown on the upper half of the keytop. (See Fig. 4-3.)

The control key (CTRL) functions as a second type of shift. When it's depressed in conjunction with another key, a character (Fig. 4-4) from a completely new set of characters appears on the screen. These "graphic" characters can be used to produce interesting pictures, designs, and graphs, either without a cartridge or with the Atari BASIC cartridge.

The RETURN key has three functions. First, it moves the printing mechanism to the left margin and down one line of the screen—again, much like a typewriter. The computer will do this for you automatically after 38 characters, even if you don't push RETURN: 38 is the greatest number of characters that will fit on a single line. The RETURN key also marks the end of a logical line for the computer. At times, it will be convenient to push RETURN at the end of each physical line, making it coincide with each logical line; at other times, the longer logical line will provide greater flexibility. Finally, the RETURN activates the computer.

The CLR.SET.TAB key operates much like the TAB key on a regular typewriter.

A number of keys perform screen-editing functions. In Fig. 4-4, these include: top row, nos. 2, 3, and 4 from the right; second row from the top, nos. 2 and 3 from the right; third row, nos. 2 and 3 from the right and no. 1 from the left; and bottom row, no. 1 from the left and right. These keys control such screen-editing functions as moving the cursor on the screen (to be discussed later) and modifying the display.

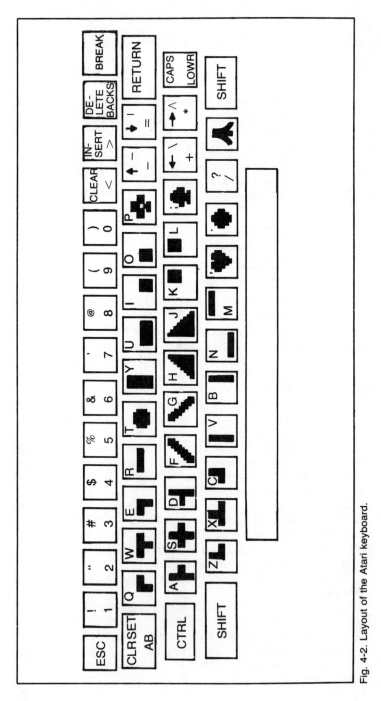

Fig. 4-2. Layout of the Atari keyboard.

60

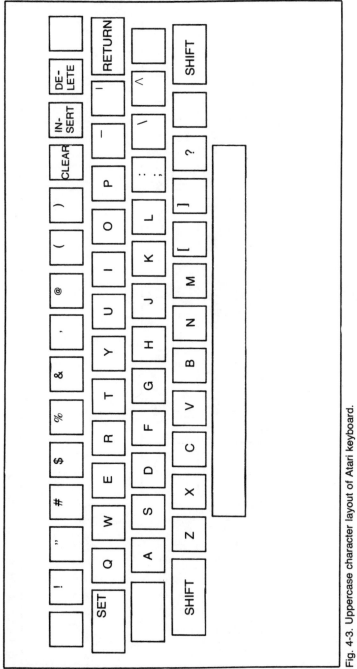

Fig. 4-3. Uppercase character layout of Atari keyboard.

61

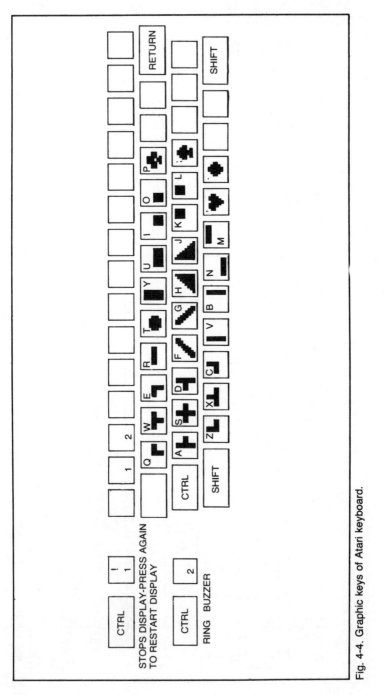

Fig. 4-4. Graphic keys of Atari keyboard.

The cursor-control function keys control the movements of the cursor; line-insert function keys create a space for a new line; character-insert function keys make space for a new character. The DELETE BACK S key erases each character as the cursor moves back one space at the time; line- and character-delete function keys remove either a whole line or a character.

A number of keys have functions not found on a regular typewriter. For example, the ESC key disables the cursor-control movements and prints a graphic character instead, while the BREAK key interrupts the computer while it's busy following instructions. This key (ノ|Ｎ) switches characters into inverse video—that is, white characters on a black background. In the "regular" mode, a keyboard creates black letters against a white background (Fig. 4-5); with inverse video, you first create a kind of black background on which you later print white characters (Fig. 4-6).

If you purchase a ready-to-use home computer, you'll receive a keyboard with it. For those who would rather build their own system by purchasing separate components—separate keyboard, terminal, computer, and other peripherals—keyboards are available from a number of companies. The RCA Model 3301 keyboard, for example, can be interfaced with a computer, and if you choose the right computer, you can add a number of peripherals—floppy disc, Winchester disc drive, printer, even a modem for use with your telephone line. This inexpensive keyboard has its own microprocessor so you can create color graphics and even music, without the use

Fig. 4-5. Regular black characters on the screen of the video display terminal. (Courtesy, Texas Instruments.)

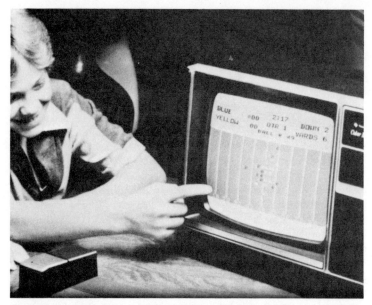

Fig. 4-6. In inverse video, a black background is first created, on which white characters are later produced. (Courtesy, Texas Instruments.)

of a computer. (All that the addition of a computer would do for you would be to let you program and add additional memory.)

DISPLAY TERMINALS

There are several ways that you can get the output from your computer onto a screen for viewing. One way is to use your regular television set; another method is by means of a video monitor; and the third way is to use a video display terminal.

Video Display Terminals

Your television set is quite adequate for general use; however, using it with your computer you can display only about 24 lines of 40 characters each; a video monitor is the best solution if you build your computer system from separate components. The video display terminal (VDT) is an integrated device—that is, a device in which the screen and keyboard are integrated into one unit. Many home/personal computers are designed that way.

The introduction of the VDT was a milestone in the development of computer systems. These display terminals are designed to display messages composed of alphanumeric characters and color graphics. (See Fig. 4-7.) Terminals have to be connected to the keyboard to generate these characters and graphics. Some manufacturers supply terminals separate from the keyboard, but a cable connection makes them integral components.

Video-display technology is based on the cathode ray tube (CRT), in which a ray of electrons is emitted from a heated cathode, focused into a fine spot, and directed toward the phosphor coating inside a glass screen. This electron beam can be electromagnetically manipulated to strike any point on the face of the screen, causing a single spot of light to appear. By moving that beam along a line, you can create the appearance of a straight line.

The electronic circuitry in a CRT causes the beam to traverse a 525-line pattern 30 times per second. (This pattern of lines is called the *raster*.) In this raster-scan technique, the electron beam moves in a regular

Fig. 4-7. Integrated keyboard and video display terminal. (Courtesy, Radio Shack, a Tandy Corp.)

pattern across the screen, synchronized with the computer, to illuminate or leave dark spots on the screen in an on-and-off sequence. These individual spots thus form on the screen a character or symbol consisting of small square dots. Since the electricity in the U.S. is based on 60 cycles per second, raster-scan displays are synchronized to 60-Hz power-line frequency; otherwise, you'd be able to see dots going on and off, which could be very hard on your eyes.

This array of square dots is called a *dot matrix*. When you read that the dot matrix is 7 by 10, it means that it consists of 7 horizontal rows of dots 10 vertical columns of dots—that is, 7 dots wide times 10 dots high. The size of the dot matrix varies from manufacturer to manufacturer.

Many VDTs display characters only in capital-letter form, and not in lowercase; only with a relatively large dot matrix can lowercase characters be suitably displayed (Fig. 4-8). Since lowercase characters have to be smaller than caps, of course, their dot matrix must also be smaller. Plus, with square dots you can't make curves, you can only suggest them. If you look at the *v, w,* and *z,* in Fig. 4-8, you'll notice that angled lines can only be shown in a staircase effect. Therefore, characters can only be made clearer by increasing the number of dots in the matrix.

Because of the interaction between your keyboard, computer, and VDT, the computer must fetch from memory a large number of dots when you fill up your screen with lines of copy. It must also cause these dots to appear on the screen in a continuous fashion, synchronized with the 60-Hz supply that's powering it. Printed information on the screen of the VDT is arranged in an orderly fashion of x number of lines by x number of characters. Many VDTs can display 24 lines on screen, with each line containing 80 characters, for a total of 1,920. If each character consists of 10 vertical dots, the computer must make 19,200 fetches per image $\times$ 60 frames/second, or 1,152,000 fetches per second!

When you depress a key on the keyboard this action generates what's called the ASCII code for that character or control signal. [The ASCII code refers to the bit pattern of the transmitted characters (see Fig. 4-9).] The resulting data signal is transmitted to the computer as input data. However, to accomplish this a "communications interface" is used. This interface can determine three modes of transmission: *simplex*, or transmission in one direction only; *half duplex*, or transmission in both directions, but not simultaneously; and *full duplex*, or simultaneous transmission in both directions.

This data can also be transmitted either synchronously and asynchronously. *Synchronous* refers to the transmission of data in a steady stream, so that the time interval between successive characters is always precisely the same; *asynchronous* means that the transmission is in irregular spurts, so that the duration of time varies between successively transmitted characters.

There's also a *message format*, which refers to the way the computer transmits data—that is, whether by character, line, or block of copy.

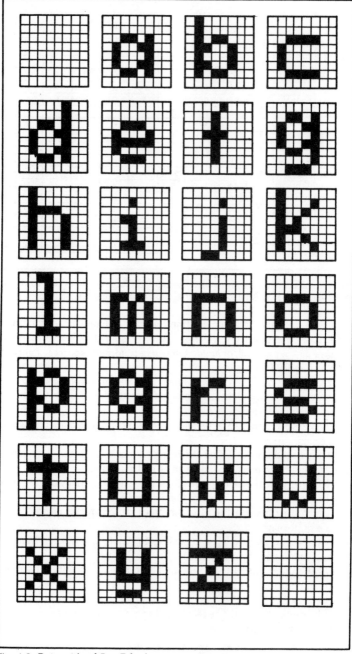

Fig. 4-8. Dot matrix of 5 × 7 for lowercase characters.

b7 b6 b5 BITS	b4	b3	b2	b1	COLUMN ROW	$0\,0\,0$ 0	$0\,0\,1$ 1	$0\,1\,0$ 2	$0\,1\,1$ 3	$1\,0\,0$ 4	$1\,0\,1$ 5	$1\,1\,0$ 6	$1\,1\,1$ 7
	0	0	0	0	0	NUL	DLE	SP	0	@	P	`	p
	0	0	0	1	1	SOH	DC1	!	1	A	Q	a	q
	0	0	1	0	2	STX	DC2	"	2	B	R	b	r
	0	0	1	1	3	ETX	DC3	#	3	C	S	c	s
	0	1	0	0	4	EOT	DC4	$	4	D	T	d	t
	0	1	0	1	5	ENQ	NAK	%	5	E	U	e	u
	0	1	1	0	6	ACK	SYN	&	6	F	V	f	v
	0	1	1	1	7	BEL	ETB	'	7	G	W	g	w
	1	0	0	0	8	BS	CAN	(	8	H	X	h	x
	1	0	0	1	9	HT	EM	)	9	I	Y	i	y
	1	0	1	0	10	LF	SUB	*	:	J	Z	j	z
	1	0	1	1	11	VT	ESC	+	;	K	[	k	{
	1	1	0	0	12	FF	FS	,	<	L	\	l		
	1	1	0	1	13	CR	GS	–	=	M	]	m	}
	1	1	1	0	14	SO	RS	.	>	N	∧	n	~
	1	1	1	1	15	SI	US	/	?	O	—	o	DEL

Fig. 4-9. ASCII code for terminals. The bit code for letter K = 100 1011, for example. (Courtesy, American National Standards Institute.)

Buffered terminals, for example, transmit data in multicharacter blocks. Incidentally, the speed by which you can transmit data is expressed in terms of bits per second, or *baud*. A speed of baud, refers to a capability of transmitting 9600 bits per second.

Depending on the keyboard, the VDT, and how your computer is programmed, you can execute a number of *screen actions*. Some of the more common actions include:

Reverse Video. Character and symbols displayed in black on a white background.

Character and/or Filed Blinking. A single character or an entire field of characters blink on and off to attract attention.

Roll (or Scroll.) All displayed lines move up or down by one line as a new line is added and an existing line is removed.

Character Insert. The capability to insert a character into an existing line of displayed text.

Character Delete. The capability to delete a character from an existing line of displayed text.

Line Insert and Line Delete. The capability to either insert or delete an entire line of text.

Erase. The capability to erase a character.

Character Repeat. The capability to repeat a character as long as the appropriate key is depressed.

There's also a strange square object on your screen called a *cursor*. The purpose of the cursor is to mark on the screen the position where the next character will be read or written from memory. You can move the cursor to the right or left, up or down. Some cursors blink, while others keep moving as long as the control key is depressed.

The keyboard/VDT combination also lets you communicate with others via the telephone lines, or to obtain data from a remote data base. In order to accomplish this, however, the VDT must have an interface that meets certain standards.

VDTs have been accepted quite well by home/personal computer users. However, they are bulky and take up a lot of space on your table or desk. To solve this problem, a number of manufacturers are working on so-called flat-panel VDTs. These new developments include ac plasma-display panels (PDPs), ac thin-film electroluminescent displays, (TFELs), vacuum-fluorescent displays (VFDs), light-emitting diodes displays (LEDs), and liquid-crystal displays, (LCDs).

PDPs—also called gas-discharge displays—are the leading challengers to the standard VDTs. PDPs have glass plates separated by a gap filled with neon gas. A thin-film conductive pattern of parallel lines is deposited on both glass surfaces in a criss-crossing pattern. Light is emitted when gas between two crossing electrodes is ionized by an electrical field. (See Fig. 4-10.)

The TFEL technology is also attracting attention, and the other developments are interesting, too. Unfortunately, though, these technologies are so new and complex that a detailed discussion of them is outside the parameters of this book.

Two other technologies do deserve some of our time, since they're in a state of development that actual production units are being built (although

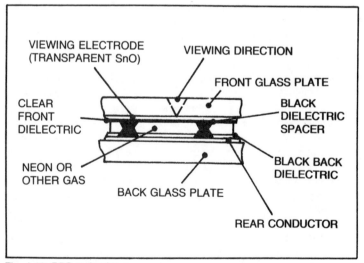

Fig. 4-10. PDP technology.

these are quite expensive at present). These two technologies are *touch-input* and *voice-input* VDTs.

Touch-Input VDTs

The industry has felt for some time that VDTs are too unwieldy and complex, and that home-computer users especially need some simple, natural communication technique in place of the often intimidating and discouraging keyboard. That's how "touch input" came about: it takes advantage of our natural instinct to point at what we want.

With a touch-input VDT you simply place your finger on the screen to transmit to the computer the data input. The sequence of actions is built around a question-and-answer technique: the computer displays both the question and the choice of responses; you simply touch the item that answers the question. (See Fig. 4-11.) There are basically four touch-input systems.

Conductive Membrane. This method involves a grid of electrons etched on two Mylar sheet membranes: one grid pattern in the X direction, and the other in the Y direction. The two membranes are mounted close to each other. Pressure on the top surface shorts a pair of electrodes, closing a conductive path. The primary element of the sensor consists of a glass sheet coated with a transparent resistive substrate. A voltage is alternately impressed along (mutually perpendicular) axes and pressure applied with the finger causes a plastic cover sheet with a transparent conductive layer to contact the resistive substrate. The voltages picked off at the point of contact are digitized to provide the numerical coordinates of the point, which are transmitted to the computer for processing.

This technique offers great accuracy; also, you can rest your finger on the point you want to touch without activating the system until you really apply pressure to the surface.

Capacitive Sensing. This system consists of a conductive substance that's actually painted on the screen: the screen is coated with a thin-film deposition that acts as a *capacitor*—a device capable of storing an electric charge. The optically clear faceplate is divided into separate touch points.

Surface-Wave Acoustics (Sonar). In this technology, a curved glass panel is mounted in the front of the VDT (Fig. 4-12). Two arrays of *piezoelectric transducers* located along the X and Y edges of the glass generate acoustic waves that move over the glass surface like ripples on a pond. (*Piezoelectric* refers to electricity produced by pressure on a nonconducting crystal; a transducer is a device that receives energy from one system retransmits it—often in a different form—to another.) A finger touching the glass reflects some of the acoustic waves back to the transducers. The X and Y coordinates of the contact point are determined electronically and transmitted to the computer controlling the display. (See Fig. 4-13.) Although the surface acoustic wave is actually a mechanical vibration, it has a microscopic amplitude and a high frequency (4 MHz [megahertz]); therefore, it's unaffected by normal vibrations or sound.

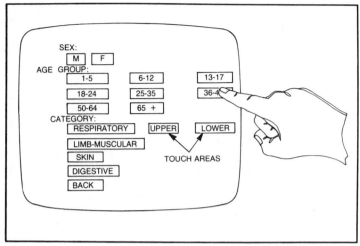

Fig. 4-11. The touch-input concept.

Scanning Infrared Beam. In this technology, infrared emitters are mounted on the left side and bottom of a printed circuit window frame. Phototransistor detectors are mounted opposite the emitters along the right side and top of the window frame. This emitter-detector arrangement produces a matrix of beams of infrared light. Each point where an X and Y beam intersects is a touch point. The window frame is mounted on the VDT, behind the bezel, so that the beams of light are parallel to and directly in front of the display surface. The window area is scanned repeatedly by sequentially pulsing the LEDs along each axis and detecting whether any beam has been interrupted (broken). Touch activation occurs whenever both the X and Y beams are broken. (See Fig. 4-14.)

Interruption of both the X and Y beams is called a "hit," and causes the system to transmit the coordinates to the host electronics. From a physical and operational point of view, the touch system divides naturally into two major parts, the opto-matrix frame and the control logic. Figure 4-15 illustrates this division. The interface between the opto-matrix and control logic is at the digital-signal level. Control signals in the form of addresses and a sample-and-hold signal (S/H) are transmitted from the control logic to the opto-matrix, while broken-beam data is transmitted from the opto-matrix to the control logic.

Whichever technology is used, simply touching a screen to read/write is a simple, virtually fault-proof method. Soon, many home computers will be equipped with such touch-input VDTs.

Voice-Input VDTs

Nothing is more exciting regarding the man/machine (computer) interface than the notion of "listening and talking computers." Many experts predict that the ability of the computer to hear and speak will enormously expand the use of computers in the home, and that as a result a fundamental change in the relationship between humans and computers is taking place. Although "touch" capitalizes on our natural instinct to point at what we want, speech is by far the more efficient mode of communication for humans.

The secret, however, lies in making the computer as proficient as we humans are in executing speech. And the problem of teaching a computer to understand a normal conversation is the toughest task of all. We use more than just sound waves to understand what we're hearing: speech recognition depends both on the context of the conversation and on the listener's knowledge of grammar, syntax, semantics—even of the speaker's personal idiosyncrasies.

No one has yet been able to devise a satisfactory computer program that incorporates these intricate abilities into some form of speech-

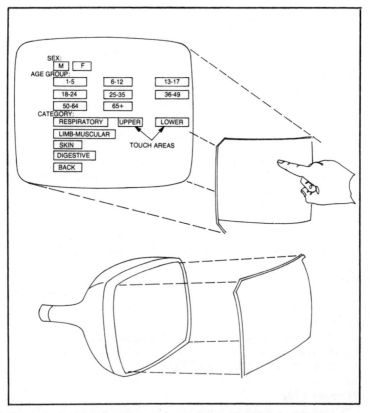

Fig. 4-12. Surface-wave acoustic technology in touch-input VDT. (Courtesy, TSD Display Products.)

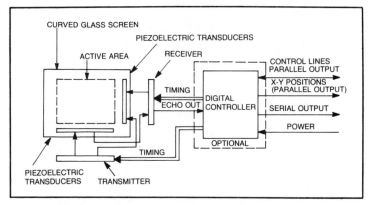

Fig. 4-13. Block diagram of surface-wave acoustic technology in touch-input VDT.

recognition system. But although much research and development still need to be done, a lot has already been accomplished.

About now, you may be wondering: Why all this fuss about talking to a computer? Well, if you think about it, the possibilities are truly exciting. The main advantage is that you don't have to be a computer expert in order to deal with a computer or handle a keyboard: you just talk, and the computer will do exactly what you tell it to do!

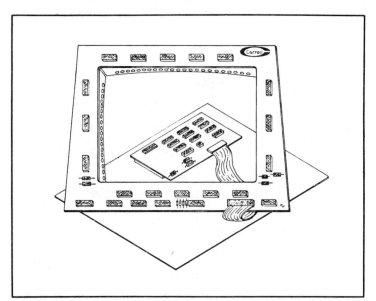

Fig. 4-14. Infrared-beam technology touch-input VDT. (Courtesy, Carroll Manufacturing.)

73

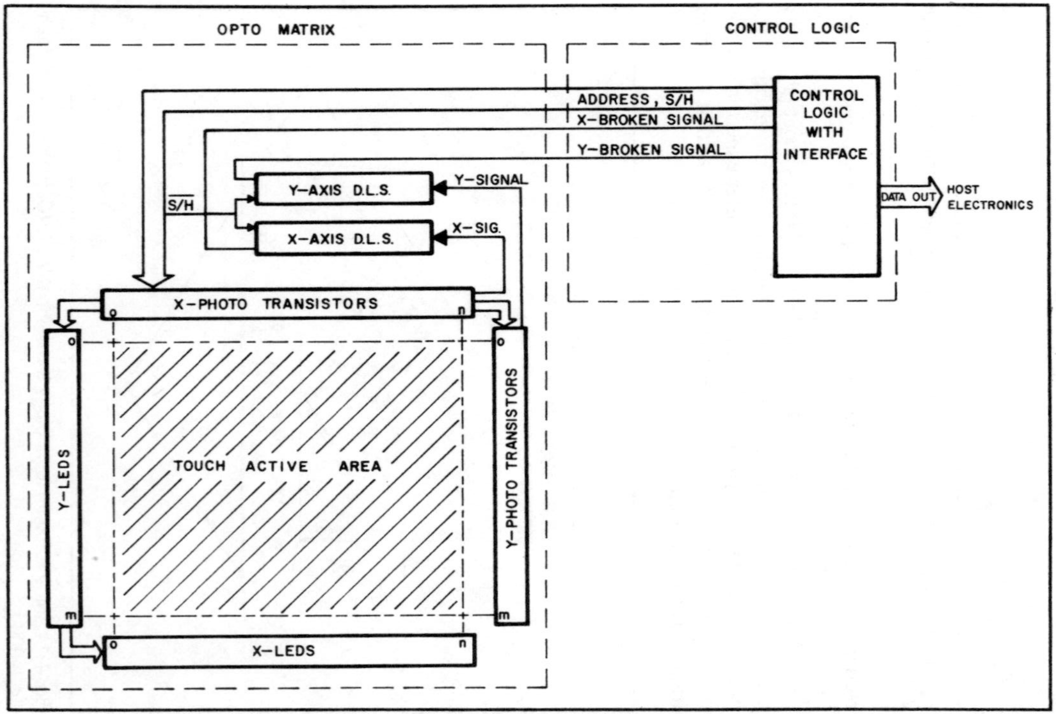

Fig. 4-15. Infrared-beam touch-input system block diagram. (Courtesy, Carroll Manufacturing.)

In the realm of man/computer interface, there are two principal considerations: voice input—or, from the point of view of the computer: *voice recognition*; and voice output, or *voice synthesis*.

VOICE RECOGNITION

Voice recognition is the ability of a computer to hear and respond to the human voice. Speech recognition implies a capability on behalf of the computer to correlate speech sounds with stored information and respond in a predictable manner. The technique operates on the premise that a voice print or pattern is as individual as a fingerprint: that is, each voice print has its own amplitude, pitch, and intensity. The computer stores these specific voice parameters and can recall them at a later time.

Synthesized speech is based on the digital storage of phonetic structures on integrated circuits. The phonetic structures are derived from phonemes, or speech sounds.

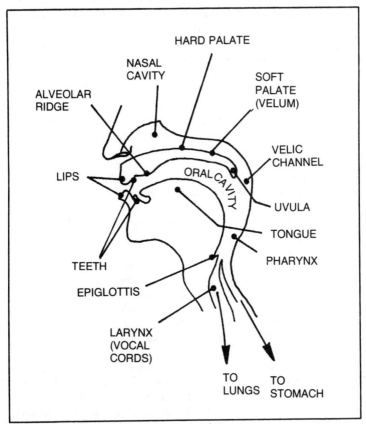

Fig. 4-16. Human vocal tract and speech system.

Before discussing the elements of speech, such as grammar, syntax, and semantics, let's take a look at the physical generator of human speech: the human vocal tract. It's a fairly important part of the body, since not only do we produce human speech here, we use the vocal tract also for purposes of eating and breathing. Our tract consists of the trachea and larynx, which in turn consists of the oral and nasal cavities. (See Fig. 4-16.) The oral cavity extends from the back of the throat to the lips, and inside it, using our lips, teeth, tongue, and soft palate, we form our speech sounds.

In the formation of speech sounds, our lungs function as a bellows, setting air in motion through the vocal tract and larynx. This flow of air through our vocal tract provides sound in different ways:

● When the vocal bands are stretched across the airflow—are brought together, so to speak—the airflow is stopped, allowing pressure to build up below the vocal bands. The pressure then forces the vocal cords apart, subsequently reducing the air pressure in the space between them. This reduction in air pressure (plus the natural elasticity of the tissues) bring the vocal cords together again. This vibration cycle is the fundamental frequency of our voice, which we hear as *pitch*.

● When the pressure built up behind the closed vocal bands is abruptly released, the burst of air allows us to pronounce such consonants, as p, k, and t.

● When a turbulence is created in the vocal tract, due to the narrow constriction in the airway, we create such sounds as f.

The generation of human speech is actually much more complex than described above, of course, since creating audible human speech brings into focus other aspects besides the generation of an airstream. There's *articulation* (modification of the airflow) and *phonation* (a process that takes place at the larynx to further modify the airstream, to mention just two. In all such actions, a number of organs have important roles: the lower lip, tongue tip, tongue blade, tongue back, upper lip, upper teeth, the bony ridge of the gums just inside the front teeth, the front of the palate behind this ridge, the center of the palate, the soft palate—each makes a contribution to the creation of speech.

The vibration, turbulence, and release of pressure (called *excitation*) cover a broad audio-frequency range. To produce the different speech sounds for each excitation mode, the broadband excitation signals are filtered by the vocal tract. The vocal tract's frequency response depends on the position of the tongue, lips, and other articulatory organs, and it is this changing shape of the tract that is the key to the different qualities of our various speech sounds.

We can generate frequencies ranging from 500 Hz to 12,000 Hz. Since these are analog signals, and since our technology is able to easily convert analog to digital, why, you might ask, is it so difficult for the computer to recognize these signals. Well, the core of the difficulty is the complex and variable way linguistic messages are encoded in speech. For example, we don't speak in i's and o's and k's: we speak in combination of these sounds called words, and—not only that—we arrange these words in still other combinations we call sentences.

And there's more: we also have 40 *phonemes*—16 vowels and 24 consonants—that are pronounced with many variations. And these phonemes are smoothly connected in speech by *diphones*, of which there are approximately 2,650! Finally, we also have to understand that phonemes can be differentiated, with each phoneme having a number of *allophones*. For example, the *p* in *penny* and the *p* in *Spain* are different allophones of the phoneme *p*. (For more information about phonemes, diphones, and allophones than space allows here you can read any of the standard texts on speech patterns.)

So, what it boils down to is that somehow the computer must learn to recognize words—and an adult may know as many as 100,000 words! But progress is being made: most available systems recognize isolated, or discrete, words, detecting word boundaries by "listening" for a minimum interval of silence between utterances. After establishing the word-boundary gap, the classifier in the system (Fig. 4-17) compares the digitally represented utterances to previously captured patterns. The spectrum analyzer in the classifier system divides the speech signals into 16 frequency bands. The coding compressor compensates for changes in the rate of articulation and reduces the spectral data generated by each utterance to a bit string of fixed length. (Unfortunately, talking in utterances, word by word, is very tiresome over any length of time.)

There are three principal coding methods; waveform digitization with compression, formant synthesis, and linear-predictive coding.

Waveform Digitization. This technique reproduces human utterances that have been recorded, analyzed, and stored either by pulse-code modulation (PCM), differential pulse-code modulation, or delta modulation.

Formant Synthesis. This method is based on natural speech. It uses phoneme synthesis in which spectral parameters are derived from basic

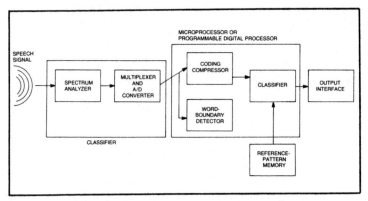

Fig. 4-17. Basic functional components of a speech-recognition device.

word sounds. (*Formants* are the vocal tract resonances that shape the spectrum of the excitation function to determine the quality and timbre of each speech sound.)

Different sounds are produced by varying the shape of the vocal tract. The spectral qualities of the speech signal, then, vary with time as the vocal tract shape varies. The acoustic signal produced by the action of the vocal tract is repeated and may be analyzed by converting it to a representation in the frequency domain (amplitude versus frequency).

Since continuous speech is generated by varying the frequencies and amplitudes of the sound sources and the frequencies of the filter—all as functions of time, which do not change rapidly—they may be digitally coded. A pulse generator in the electronic circuit whose middle frequencies are varied through filters is used. The frequency and amplitude of the periodic voice-excitation pulses are controlled logically, as are the frequency range and amplitude of the *frication*, or noise, generator for the f, s, v, and z sounds. Three filters whose middle frequencies correspond roughly with the frequency response of the mouth are also used. The pulse excitation passes through a simulated nasal resonator, which introduces characteristics of such sounds as m and n, which are produced as the mouth cavity opens into the nasal cavity.

Linear-Predictive Coding. This process is similar to formant synthesis, with the exception that the sound signal must determine present filter coefficients, with the quality of synthesis improving as the number of coefficients increases.

VOICE OUTPUT

The technique of voice output, in which the computer talks without listening to what you have to say, is much further advanced than voice input. The reasons are simple: the designer has time to record different voices, produce them digitally, and store them in the computer's memory. The programmer also has the opportunity to select the words deemed necessary. By comparison, the voice recognition discussed earlier requires that the microprocessor recognize and react to what is said, at least to the point of being able to match a vocal input with the proper entry in its own programmed vocabulary.

Speech synthesis, or voice output, is therefore much easier to handle and implement (although it's still a complex technology). Electronic games, for one example, have successfully utilized speech synthesis. Some systems use *synthesis by rule*, where voice signals are first recorded according to parameters that attempt to capture the essence of phonemes, and then produced according to a set of rules. Others use the technique of *playback of recorded utterances*, where words or phrases are selected in order by the controlling processor and then played back sequentially, stringing together coherent messages, a method also called *synthesis by concatenation*.

A number of personal/home computer manufacturers—including Texas Instruments, Radio Shack, Pet-Commodore, and Ohio Scientific—

Fig. 4-18. Speech-synthesis module. (Courtesy, Telesensory Systems.)

offer speech synthesis. The Texas Instruments speech module has about 300 words in its memory, and new words can be formed by combining different words. For example, since the words "there" and "four" are in the memory, the word "therefore" can be constructed by combining them.

Some companies, such as Maryland Computer Services and Telesensory Systems, manufacture computer and related products that talk to the blind and handicapped. Still other concerns supply speech-recognition and speech-synthesis modules, either for specific use or for use with personal/home computers. There are special modules that interface with the computer. (See Fig. 4-18.)

GRAPHIC DISPLAYS

As we learned earlier, a VDT—whether color or monochrome—is basically a character-oriented display that includes several additional writing and coordinate positioning modes. A graphic display, on the other hand, is a VDT with the additional capability of being able to generate, via the keyboard and computer, lines (vectors), curves, and other special patterns.

A number of personal/home computers can generate graphics, using a number of techniques. One such technique is called direct-view storage tube (DVST), where a picture is drawn by a directed electron beam, causing the image to be traced on an extremely long-persistence phosphor inside the CRT (Fig. 4-19). However, the beam writes on a fine mesh grid mounted just behind the phosphor-coated screen (rather than on the phosphor itself). The written points, excited by the electrons, continue to glow and emit light after the beam stops writing; the image remains visible until the entire screen is erased.

79

This technique is not used in home computers, however. The bit-mapped raster-scan technique is most commonly used in personal/home computers (Fig. 4-20). Image data are stored in a large memory—the bit map—with each bit (or byte, in the case of displays with color or gray levels) corresponding to an addressable point on the screen. A beam from the CRT constantly scans the face of the screen, which is divided into strips of equal size called *scan lines*. Each strip, in turn, is divided into blocks of equal size, called *picture elements*, or simply *pixels*. The beam scans each line, controlling the intensity of each pixel by means of the information stored in memory (Fig. 4-22). Each vertical scan takes 1/60 of a second.

The scan is referred to as *interlaced* if it takes two vertical passes to complete one frame—the odd lines being drawn on pass one, and the even lines on pass two. If the entire picture is drawn in a single pass, the scan is said to be *noninterlaced*. Interlacing allows the refresh rate to be half of what would ordinarily be necessary to prevent screen flicker.

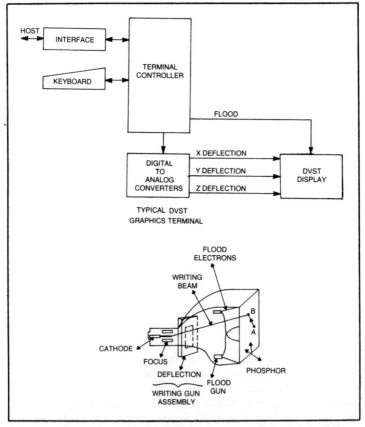

Fig. 4-19. Direct-view storage tube (DVST) technique of creating graphics.

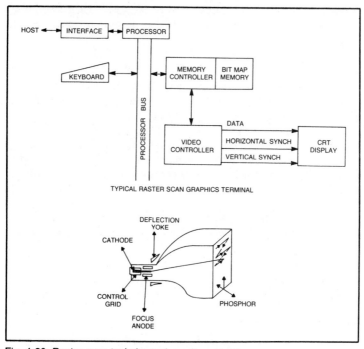

Fig. 4-20. Raster-scan technique of creating graphics.

The screen uses three colors of phosphor, and offers an almost un-limited palette of different colors and gray scale values—more than 2 million! In addition, a broad range of brightness levels is possible by varying the intensity of the electron beam. Truly, raster scan has brought with it a wide range of screen resolutions.

Many displays have what amounts to a *vector and/or raster mode*. In the vector mode, *XY* coordinates define the end points of a line (Fig. 4-21). Images are analyzed in terms of straight lines, and curves become short straight-line segments. In the raster mode, pictures are broken into small cells.

In specifications, *spatial resolution* refers to the product of the number of horizontal pixels times the number of vertical pixels. *Color resolution* is the number of bits per pixel, and depends on the number of color/intensity choices possible at each pixel. A graphics system with 256 times 256 times 4 bits resolution has a total of 65,536 pixels, each of which can display 2^4 (or 16) color/intensity variations.

What about three-dimensional graphics? Well, we're all waiting for 3-D television, and when that becomes an inexpensive consumer item video graphics in 3-D will almost certainly follow. A technique has been developed for 3-D graphics in which a vibrating mirror turns a series of two-dimensional images from a CRT screen into a continuous 3-D image. This system has proved to be a major step towards the goal 3-D graphics, but it will probably be a while before it's economically feasible for you, as a computer owner, to own such a device.

THE HARD-COPY TERMINAL OR PRINTER

A printer is a device that prints out the information you have processed by means of your keyboard through the computer and VDT. It provides you with what's called *hard copy*—information on paper.

Why on paper, you may ask, if a computer is supposed to be a device for eliminating paperwork? Well, you sometimes want to have a permanent record of what's in the computer's memory. Also, an application program in RAM can only be processed through your cassette recorder or disc drive(s); if you borrow such a program from somebody else, you can retain it for your own uses thanks to hard copy.

Printers are classified according to the imaging technology used, as either *serial* or *line*; either *solide* or *matrix*; and either *impact* or *nonimpact*.

Serial Printers

Serial printers generate one character at a time, in terms of characters per second (cps).

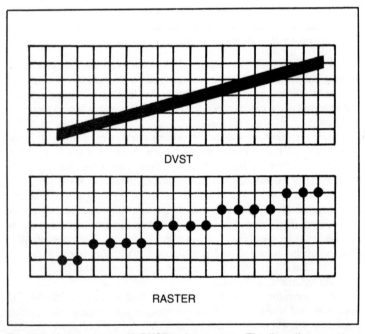

Fig. 4-21. Vectors drawn with DVST and raster scan. The discontinuous nature of raster vector is known as stair-stepping.

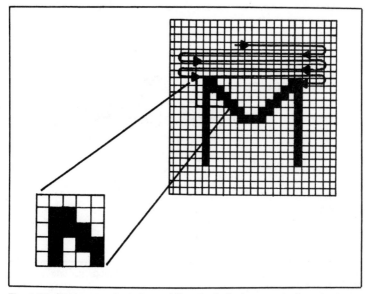

Fig. 4-22. Raster-scan technique of "burning" pixels on and off as the beam moves back and forth down the display surface. The diagonal vectors are stair-stepped pixels.

Solid Printing (Serial). Also called "formed" printing, solid printing (serial mode) produces whole solid images at one time. The character to be printed is selected from an array of moving-type elements, such as an IBM Selectric type ball, a daisy wheel, or a thimble.

In a system like the daisy wheel, the printing mechanism consists of a steel or plastic disc that rotates in a circle, moving the proper fingerlike implement to a place where the print hammer can strike it (Fig. 4-23). Typical print speeds for daisy-wheel mechanisms range from 30 to 80 characters per second. The printing mechanism can be easily removed, permitting the use of different *fonts* (styles and sizes of "type").

Matrix Printing (Serial). This technique creates the desired image by selectively placing stroke segments (usually dots) on the form. A dot-matrix printing mechanism doesn't rotate, but rather prints in place by means of a vertical array of needlelike wires—typically, seven to nine per vertical array. The characters to be printed are stored in ROM, which then determines which printing needles in the array are to strike the ribbon and imprint the character on the printing medium. (See Fig. 4-24.)

In addition, the two vertical columns of needlelike elements permit the printing of 5 × 7, 7 × 7, or 7 × 9 dot arrays. The more wire needles the unit has, the more closely the printing mechanism can approximate the print quality of fully formed characters. Therefore, this type of printer is excellent for creating graphics.

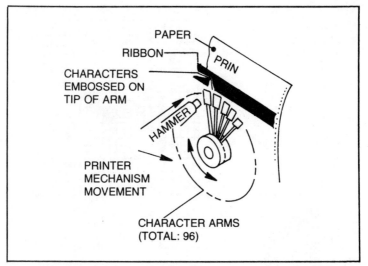

Fig. 4-23. The daisy-wheel method of solid serial printing. (Courtesy, Data-products Corporation.)

Impact Printing (Serial). The impact process—the traditional way to transfer ink to paper—involves the rapid compression of paper, type element, and inked ribbon. The typewriter is of course the typical example.

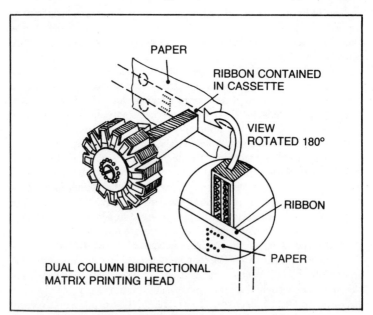

Fig. 4-24. Matrix printing method (serial).

Impact printers press the character element (or wire) against the inked ribbon, thereby making an impression on the front of the paper.

Nonimpact Printing (Serial). The nonimpact (NIP) processes are subdivided into plain and coated-paper technologies. This is not the place to get into an examination of pulp and paper methodology, so we'll settle for listing a few of the technologies. Two of those using plain paper are the ink-jet process, in which droplets of ink are directed to the paper; and electrophotography, which uses a laser writing on a drum. The coated-paper processes include such technologies as thermal (heat writing on thermally sensitive paper); electrosensitive (electric charges burns off thin metallic coating to reveal black undercoat); and electrostatic, or dielectric, in which the coated paper is first selectively charged by a stylus and then passes through a toner that's attracted by the charge area.

Nonimpact printers create matrix images, and the most common nonimpact mechanism is the thermal-matrix printer. The printhead moves across the print line, forming characters by heating chemically treated paper at the desired locations (Fig. 4-25). Print rates typically range from 20 to 120 cps, with good print quality.

The electrosensitive-matrix printer (Fig. 4-26) uses alumi- num-coated paper that changes color when a voltage is applied. The print- head houses electrodes that are pulsed when a dot is to be formed. The charge goes through the paper to a metal plate (common ground) behind the paper completing the current path. Print rates range from 150 to 200 cps with good quality.

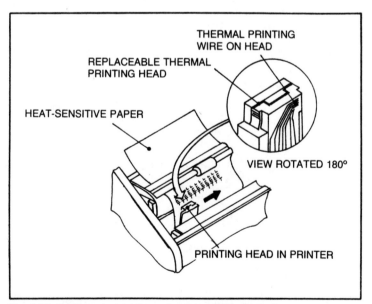

Fig. 4-25. Nonimpact serial thermal-matrix printing method.

Line Printers

Line printers form characters in entire parallel lines, one line at a time, and are rated in terms of lines per minute (lpm). This is an obvious contrast with the serial printers first discussed, which generate only one *character* at a time.

Solid Printing (Line). This process uses a type-element array, such as a drum, chain, train, cylinder, belt, or band. (See Fig. 4-27.)

Matrix Printing (Line). Shuttle matrix printers are typified by a shuttle comb or bank of print elements and microprocessor electronics. Speed ranges from 126 to 600 lpm. Helix matrix line printers have a speed range of from 300 to 500 lpm; multi-head matrix printers have multiple arrays of solenoid-operated wire print elements, with speeds of 50 to 400 lpm.

Impact Printing (Line). Impact line printers include band, drum, and chain printers that trigger a hammer, which in turn forces the paper from behind against the ribbon and a moving-type element.

The drum printer (Fig. 4-28) has a complete set of characters embossed against the circumference of a horizontally rotating steel drum.There are one full set of characters and one hammer for each print position. Characters to be printed are transferred to a receive-data memory, one line at a time. The data memory is scanned and coupled to the rotating drum. As the character to be printed rotates into position, a hammer-fire signal is issued; the hammer strikes the paper, forcing it into

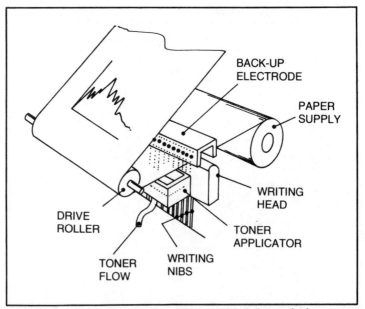

Fig. 4-26. Nonimpact serial electrosensitive-matrix printing method.

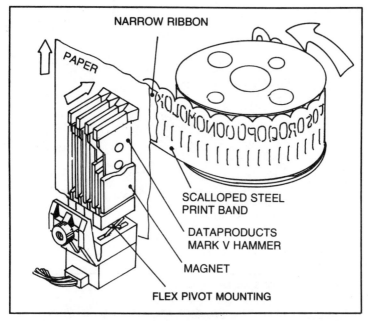

NARROW RIBBON

SCALLOPED STEEL
PRINT BAND

DATAPRODUCTS
MARK V HAMMER

MAGNET

FLEX PIVOT MOUNTING

PAPER

Fig. 4-27. Solid line printer using band technology.

the ribbon and drum. The print rate for this mechanism, which can exceed 300 cps, is determined by a combination of drum speed, character set size, paper movement time, and data transfer rate. Print quality is good.

In cylinder printing (Fig. 4-29) the cylinder print mechanism rotates along a vertical axis on a moveable carriage that traverses a line to the

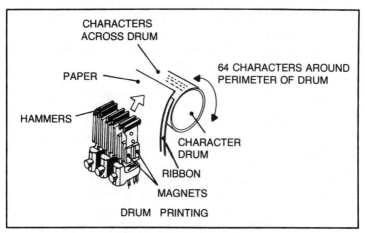

CHARACTERS
ACROSS DRUM

PAPER

64 CHARACTERS AROUND
PERIMETER OF DRUM

HAMMERS

CHARACTER
DRUM

RIBBON

MAGNETS

DRUM PRINTING

Fig. 4-28. Impact matrix line printer using drum technology.

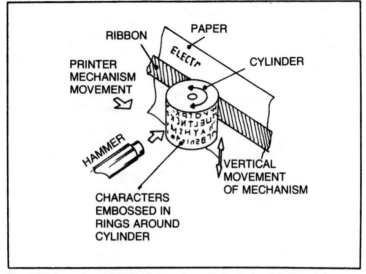

Fig. 4-29. Impact matrix line printer using cylinder technology.

desired print position. The cylinder has several rings of full characters embossed on its surface, making up the printable character set. When the carriage is positioned, the cylinder is rotated and then raised or lowered to bring the appropriate character in position for the cylinder to strike the ribbon and form the printed character. Speed is slow—only about 10 cps.

Nonimpact Printing (Line). Nonimpact line printers follow the same technologies as those described earlier in the serial printer category.

Comparison of Printers

There are disadvantages and advantages to each of the printing techniques mentioned. If line printers, for example, aren't adjusted properly, these units can cause line smear or character misregistration. Vertically moving fonts, such as drums, can produce vertical misregistration or wavy lines; horizontally moving fonts, such as bands and belts, can cause horizontal misregistration, or uneven spacing between the characters on a line.

Serial matrix printers, on the other hand, may be unsuitable when important correspondence or formal text preparation is required. Nonetheless, some nonimpact matrix printers provide such fine resolution that the characters appear fully formed.

So, whether the unit you choose prints fully formed or matrix characters, it's up to you to make sure that the resulting print quality is suitable for *your* application. You can always request print samples before you make your choice, so that you can check for clear, sharp characters that have no extraneous ink, smudging, or background clutter.

Another important consideration, of course, is speed. Basically, three factors are involved here: print rate, throughput, and input data rate. The *print rate*, measured in cps, tells how many characters can be placed on the paper in a second; *throughput* refers to the number of lines printed per minute; and *input data rate*, finally, relates to the interfacing of the printer with your computer.

There are three interfacing methods: 8-bit parallel; RS-232C; and Centronics-compatible. Of the three, RS-232C is most commonly used on personal/home computers. Regardless of interface type, however, the input data rate relates how fast the printer can process characters and therefore determines how frequently the printer and computer must "handshake."

Directly related to a printer's "intelligence" is its ability to print graphics and to perform plotting functions. Graphics are very important now that many home computer systems offer the capability of printing them.

Noise may be yet another consideration. Impact printers generally exhibit noise figures ranging from 50 dBa (adjusted decibels) to as high as 75 dBa. The worst offenders are dot-matrix printers, primarily because their heads make a buzzing sound. But this is something you can probably live with. (You can always cover the unit with a noise-dampening cover.)

Serial impact dot-matrix printers are most commonly used in home computers, because the mechanism has the inherent accuracy to place dots anywhere on the paper. This makes them excellent devices for multipurpose use, including copy and graphics.

Figure 4-30 shows a line printer that uses a single-hammer system and a platen with a series of raised ridges. The carriage movement, the motion of the hammer, and the revolution of the platen are minutely synchronized. Figure 4-31 illustrates the mechanical construction of the hammer, platen, and dot sensor, and Fig. 4-32 shows the relationship between the hammer, the position of the printed dot, and the dot-sensor signal.

The ridges on the platen are set for ten dots, which is the height of one column. (The top and bottom dots are not for printing, but for spacing between the lines.) While the platen rotates for each ridge, seven dot signals are sent to the hammer head. Each signal activates or deactivates the head, according to the command being executed. The head is activated and deactivated separate times while one ridge passes by the hammer head. (The hammer head is slanted to compensate for the constant rightward motion of the head position.)

Each pass of a ridge causes one column to be printed. Since there are 18 ridges on the platen, 18 columns (three characters) are printed for each revolution of the platen. In the graphic mode, 8-bit data is used to address each dot in a seven-dot column. The first bit of the eight is always 1, to tell the printer that the data is for the graphic mode.

Figure 4-33 illustrates a thermal printer. With this printer, 5×7 dot-matrix characters are printed one at a time—serially—as received on 5.5 inch-wide paper at ten characters and six lines per inch.

Fig. 4-30. Typical line printer. (Courtesy, Radio Shack.)

The *Serial Impact Dot-Matrix Printer* in Fig. 4-34 consists of a print head with 7 solenoid-operated print wires. The print head is moved across the printing area by a shoe that engages in the slot of a cylindrical cam. This single-groove cam ensures vertical linearity by eliminating the crossovers found in a multi-groove cam. (See Fig. 4-35.)

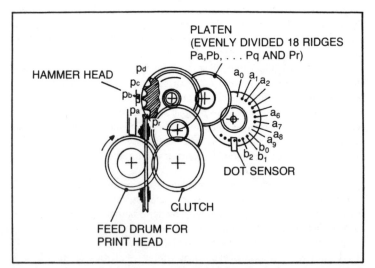

Fig. 4-31. Mechanical construction and relationship of hammer, platen, and dot sensor of line printer.

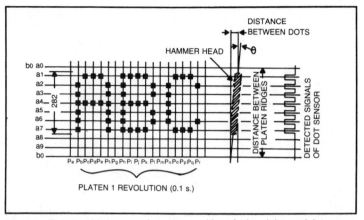

Fig. 4-32. Relationship between hammer, position of printed dot, and dot-sensor signal.

Two stepper motors drive the print mechanism: one is used for moving the print head, while the other is used to advance the paper. The two motors operate independently and are controlled by the microprocessor.

As to the method of paper feeding, the purchaser can select either a pressure roller driving the paper with friction, or tractors (Fig. 4-36). Paper can be fanfold (with or without tractor holes), rolls, or single sheets (Fig. 4-37). Optional roll-paper holders and single-sheet feeder assemblies assist in using these paper forms. An ink ribbon self-contained in a cartridge, is easily replaced without opening the printer case.

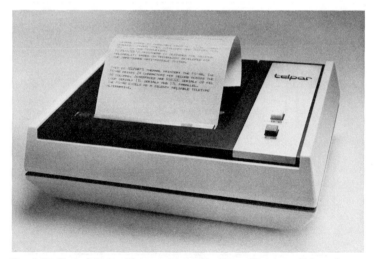

Fig. 4-33. Typical thermal impact dot-matrix printer. (Courtesy, Telspar.)

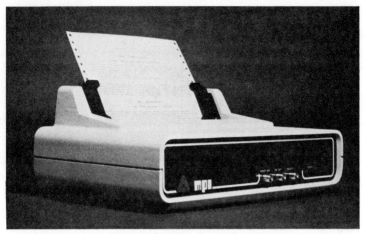

Fig. 4-34. Serial impact dot-matrix printer. (Courtesy, Microperipherals Inc.)

Figure 4-38 gives you an idea of the kind of graphic effects a serial impact dot-matrix printer is capable of.

DIGITIZERS

Another accessory often used with personal/home computers is the *digitizer*, which allows you to process hand-drawn graphics and text through the computer and print them on your printer (Fig. 4-39). It's something like a drafting board, except that the digitizer is computerized.

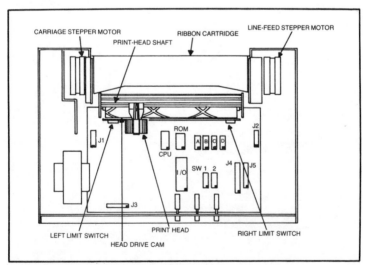

Fig. 4-35. Print mechanism of serial impact dot-matrix printer.

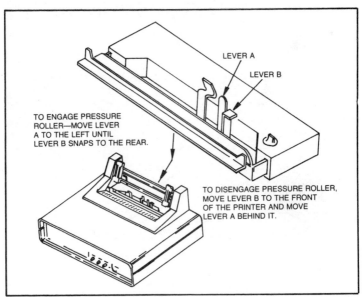

Fig. 4-36. Selectable paper feeding.

A basic digitizer consists of a tablet and *stylus* (a penlike device) and the necessary built-in electronic circuitry. The principles of operation are quite similar to the touch-sensitive input technology described earlier in the section on VDTs. The stylus interrupts X and Y coordinates, and the location of this interruption is transmitted in digital form to the computer. It's displayed on the screen, and—if desired—transmitted to the printer.

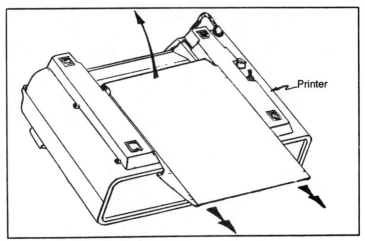

Fig. 4-37. Single-sheet paper feeding.

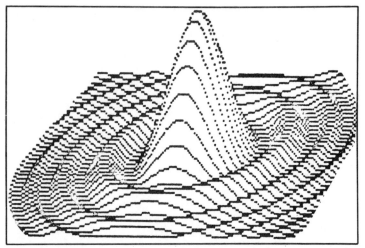

Fig. 4-38. Combination of text and graphics printed with a serial impact dot-matrix printer.

Types of Digitizers

Several different technologies are used to manufacture digitizers.

Sonic. In this technology, a sound pulse generated by the stylus is detected by the X and Y axis, transferred into digital form, and sent to the computer.

Magnetostrictive. A grid of magnetic wires is imbedded in the tablet and a current is pulsed through these wires. The stylus picks these pulses up, and they are then transmitted to the computer.

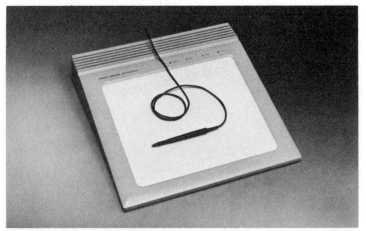

Fig. 4-39. A typical digitizer, the HP 9111. Graphics Tablet from Hewlett-Packard. (Courtesy, Hewlett-Packard.)

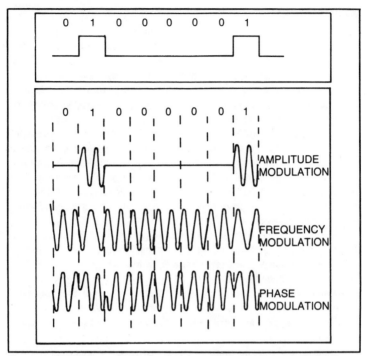

Fig. 4-40. Digital transmission (*top*) and modulation techniques (*bottom*).

Direct Magnetostrictive. This process is similar to the technique above, except that the wires are made of copper and the signal is generated by the stylus rather than by the wires. A microprocessor develops the digital coordinates.

Digitizer Mode

There are two modes of digitizer operation.

Point Mode. When switched to this mode the drawing placed on the digitizer is transmitted to the computer point by point.

Stream Mode. This mode is used for continuous drawing: as long as the stylus is pressed against the tablet, the data continues to be transmitted to the computer.

When you buy a digitizer, a key consideration is *resolution*, which refers to the smallest unit of movement that can be detected by the digitizer output. A digitizer with a resolution of 400 lines per inch, for example, has 400 × 400, or 160,000, distinguishable coordinates within a one-inch-square area. If the size of the digitizer were 11 inches by 11 inches, you'd have a total of 19,360,000 addressable locations!

A digitizer interfaces with the computer through the standard serial interface RS-232C, or the IEEE-488.

MODEMS

Modem stands for *modulator/demodulator*. It's the device that links your computer over the telephone lines with other computers or with such commercial data bases as The Source, CompuServe, and others. Because the telephone transmits signals in analog form, whereas the computer transmits in digital form, in order for your computer to use the telephone lines you need a peripheral capable of translating from digital to analog (and vice versa). That's where the modem comes in.

The telephone's analog transmission is continuous, with the electrical signal in the form of continuous, constantly varying wave lengths. Digital transmission, on the other hand, is discontinuous, made up of pulsating on/off signals. The human voice, with its vast range of tones, lends itself naturally to transmission using continuously variable signals. But computer data, whose bits are composed of electrical pulses signifying either a 1 or a 0, requires discontinuous, on/off transmission of electrical signals.

Modems change voltage pulses into something that travels better on the phone network. At low speeds a shift-keying technique is used, where 0s are changed into pulses of a given frequency and 1s into pulses of another frequency a few hundred hertz away. At higher speeds, frequency shifting is augmented with phase shifting, while at still higher speeds the modulation methods include a certain amount of bit encoding, some advanced techniques of amplitude modulation, and phase and frequency modulation (Fig. 4-40).

In amplitude modulation the volume of the carrier signal is varied, so that one volume represents a 0 and another a 1. In frequency modulation on the other hand, a frequency represents a 0 and an increased frequency a 1. In phase modulation the rhythm of the carrier signal is altered.

Another thing to consider is telephone-line transmission is that, while your 8-bit computer deals with such transmission one byte at a time, the phone line doesn't have eight wires to devote to carrying each bit of that byte. Therefore, only one bit at a time, one after the other, can be transmit-

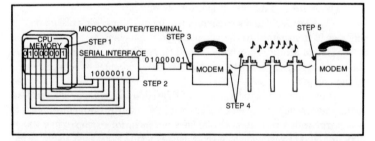

Fig. 4-41. The 8-bit message of the computer is transmitted to the interface, which transfers the eight bits to a serial, one-bit-at-a-time transmission. The modem translates the digital signal into an analog one suitable for transmission over the phone lines. The second modem retranslates the analog signal back into digital format.

Fig. 4-42. Typical acoustic coupler modem. (Courtesy, Novation Inc.)

ted. Consequently, the parallel configuration of the 8-bit system has to be transferred to a serial mode. (See Fig. 4-41.)

There are two modes of transmission: asynchronous and synchronous. In asynchronous transmission, the time interval between characters varies; it's used for low-speed transfer, as from your terminal to The Source or CompuServe. Synchronous transmission uses line capabilities more efficiently but requires more complex circuitry with consequently higher cost.

Fig. 4-43. Typical hard-wired modem. (Courtesy, Radio Shack.)

Another thing to consider is the direction of the transmission. There are three direction modes: Simplex, which is a broadcast similar to that used by a TV station. It's a signal sent out in all directions without expecting a response.

Half duplex which is similar to citizen's band (CB) operations, for example, where only one signal at a time can be transmitted—from A to B, or back from B to A.

Full duplex, in which both ends of the line can transmit and receive simultaneously.

Two types of modems are available: *acoustic couplers* and *hard-wired modems*. An acoustic coupler (Fig. 4-42) changes the digital signals from the computer into acoustical tones that can be transmitted through the mouthpiece of the telephone. This type of modem is less expensive, but a disadvantage is that background noise from your computer room can be picked up by the coupler and interfere with the transmission.

A hard-wired modem (Fig. 4-43) connects directly to the telephone by means of a telephone plug.

If you read the specifications of a modem you'll often see the phrase "Originate/answer modes." Most good modems have this capability of switching between these modes. This is necessary because, when you dial up The Source or CompuServe, for example, you are the "originator" - i.e., the one requesting information. Your modem will thus have to be set in the Originate mode, while The Source or CompuServe are set in the Answer mode (since they're answering by transmitting the requested information).

Fig. 4-44. Condenser microphone to replace carbon mic in telephone to achieve better signal-to-noise ratio. (Courtesy, Novation Inc.)

Table 4-1. RS-232C Pin Connections

Pin number	Mnemonic	Description
1	AA	Protective ground
2	BA	Transmitted data
3	BB	Received data
4	CA	Request to send
5	CB	Clear to send
6	CC	Data set ready
7	AB	Signal ground [common return]
8	CF	Received line signal detector
9	—	Reserved for data set testing
10	—	Reserved for data set testing
11	—	Unassigned
12	SCF	Sec. rec'd line signal detector
13	SCB	Sec. clear to send
14	SBA	Secondary transmitted data
15	DB	Receiver signal element timing—DCE source
16	SBB	Secondary received data
17	DD	Receiver signal element timing—DCE source
18	—	Unassigned
19	SCA	Secondary request to send
20	CD	Data terminal ready
21	CG	Signal quality detector
22	CE	Ring indicator
23	CH/CI	Data signal rate selector—DTE/DCE source
24	DA	Transmit sign element timing—DTE source
25	—	Unassigned

Note, however, that although your modem is in the Originate mode, it's still able to receive data. When you originate, your modem sends a signal on frequency "A" for the bit 1 and "A+" for the bit 0. Your modem will also use a range of frequencies "B" ("B" and "B+") to receive data. The computer at the other end (The Source or CompuServe, for example) is set to receive your request on frequencies "A" and "A+," and to send the information on frequencies "B" and "B+".

Note: A company named Novation has recently solved the problem of acoustic transmission by designing a condenser microphone (Fig. 4-44) that can easily replace the carbon microphone of your telephone. This solid-state device has an integrated circuit preamplifier that maintains constant line levels and improves signal-to-noise ratio; plus, it's approved by the Federal Communications Commission (FCC). (Any item that's used in the telephone network has to be certified by the FCC as meeting telephone network standards.)

We've already mentioned the "RS-232C" standard. This standard was devised to allow consistency in the transmission of signals. According to this standard, each data set has a standard 25-pin connector, and each pin in that connector has to be wired exactly the same in each computer and peripheral. Table 4-1 lists the assigned connections.

Chapter 5
Personal/Home
Computers

As computer terminology expands, it gets more and more difficult to differentiate between micro-, personal, home, mini-, supermini-, midi-, or
mainframe computers.

With such a profusion of terms, how can we be sure we're all talking
about the same thing? For example, what's a personal computer and what's a
home computer? Let's see if we can clear up this issue anyhow:

TERMINOLOGY

A *personal computer* is any programmable computing device that's
privately used by a single person. It can be used for everything from learning
programming and solving complex engineering problems to keeping track of
the family checkbook and playing games. When used primarily at the individual's home, for the use of other members of the family as well as himself, a
personal computer is often called a *home computer*. Although some manufacturers label their units home computers, elsewhere in the industry
they're categorized as personal microcomputer. In this book we've sought a
middle ground by combining the terms to make *personal/home computer*.

Literally speaking, though, there's really no such things yet as a home
computer, that is a computer designed solely for personal, household applications. Although educational and industrial applications for personal computers are growing rapidly, we have yet to see the true home-computer
market open up. Most people who have computers in their home use them
for business applications, or as part of a hobby—and these applications,
pleasant as they may be, don't begin to utilize a computer in its full sense.

The reason that a real home-computer package hasn't come on the
scene yet is the lack of software—that is, of application programs. A
number of small, simple systems are available that even the greenest

consumer will find easy to use, but a real package—a full-grown system that you simply plug in and then, by means of simple wire connections, computerize your house with—hasn't been developed yet. (A number of computerized homes have been built, and they will be discussed later.)

This doesn't mean you can't computerize your home today. You can, by choosing from the modules and accessories available on the market today, and building your own! (It's not as hard as it may sound.) This book has been specifically written to help those who may have been apprehensive about venturing into their own home-computing device, to encourage them to start playing with those bits. This chapter especially, as well as those that precede and follow it, should help you make sense out of what's sold today in the way of personal/home computers.

At this point I feel I must acknowledge the Ohio Scientific Corporation's generosity in lending me a $3,000 computer system to work with in compiling this book. It certainly proved to me that there's nothing complicated or frightening about working with computers.

Personal computing no longer requires that you be totally familiar with electronics and computer science in order to "get your feet wet," computer-wise. Complete off-the-shelf systems are sold in numerous computer stores and department stores. A certain familiarity with the subject is recommended, of course—at least enough savvy that you're able to recognize what a personal/home computer can do generally, and can do for you specifically.

Just what is a *microcomputer*? It's a small, relatively low-cost computer that manipulates words that are 8 bits long. (Remember 8 bits equal a byte.) A word can represent a character of text, two decimal digits, or an instruction. Some more expensive systems have a 16-bit word capacity.

Although a personal computer is typically a general-purpose, standalong microprocessor-based system that relies on conversational interaction between it and you, the operator, it's difficult to compare personal computer systems. Some manufacturers package the keyboard, VDT, computer, and floppy-disc drives in a single unit; others sell all the parts separately, like the components of a stereo system. Prices vary, too, according to capability, degree of sophistication, and ruggedness.

The microprocessor in a personal/home computer is often an Intel 8080-compatible Zilog Z80, a Motorola 6800, or an MOS-technology 6052. Built-in RAM memories range in size from 4 kB (kilobytes) to as much as 64 kB. (48 kB represent about 8,000 words of English text.) Additional peripherals are abundantly available. For example, most personal/home systems permit the use of a cassette recorder for program and data storage, or a 5¼- or 8-inch floppy disc. Some have the capability for adding on a hard-disc drive.

With all these options available, how do you intelligently select the computer that best fits your needs? There are so many systems on the market, that this is a difficult question to resolve with a flat answer. On the other hand, once you realize that you're not so much interested in a computer per se, but more in *what you want the computer to do for you*, the problem of choosing the right system begins to get easier. Defining your needs is all-important.

HOME COMPUTER CAPABILITIES

Following is a list of some of the areas in which your personal computer can help, inform, and entertain you in your home:

- Games
- Education (learning)
- Home-energy control
- Security
- Appliance control
- Home bookkeeping (financing, budgeting, tax preparation, recordkeeping)
- Medical supplies control
- Information center
- Communication
- Music
- Cartoons/art
- Investment analysis
- Recipes
- Message logs
- Word processing
- Telephone answering
- Property inventory

and lots more.

Personal computers are also getting smarter, and their manufacturers are, too: the latter are paying careful attention to the expectations of these machine's users and potential users—that's you and I! They're working hard to provide more software, for one thing, and making smaller, easier to handle computers for another.

BUILD YOUR OWN!

There's more than one way to acquire a computer. Building your own from a kit is one of them. Kits are usually less expensive than the comparable fully assembled systems, plus they offer a unique opportunity to develop a thorough knowledge and understanding of how a computer works.

A wide choice of single-board computers (SBCs) is available, such as the MOS-technology KIM (keyboard interface module), Synertek's SYM, and boards from Motorola, Texas Instruments, and others. The MOS-technology KIM board is probably the one most widely used, and a great deal of software and add-ons are available for it. It uses a calculator-type keyboard for command entry. You can program the microprocessor yourself by direct entry of hexadecimal machine-code commands; the data readout is a simple numeric display. Most SBCs allow the use of such add-ons as a cassette recorder, as well as expansion of the memory. You can also add a printer for hard-copy output.

Programming these devices is quite a primitive affair, since the amount of on-board memory is very small. However, with some SBCs you can add on-board RAM memory, while with others a buffered memory-expansion board must be used. Whatever its parameters, a single-board computer offers you enough expansions to make your original SBC the computer card for a full-feature microprocessor system.

A step up from the "bare-bones" SBC just described is the Rockwell AIM microcomputer system. This single-board, 6502 microprocessor computer comes with an added typewriter-style keyboard, a single-line display, and a built-in printer. Add-ons for the AIM include a case, power supply, and assembler, plus BASIC and FORTH packages in firmware. For a full-feature system, an expansion card cage and a mother board are available. (This unit is more fully described in the next chapter.)

Another class of single-board computer is the Cosmac VIP by RCA. This microprocessor-based unit has a calculator-type keyboard for data input and displays its data output on a Television set. This unit is also more fully described in the next chapter.

COMPLETE (FULLY ASSEMBLED) SYSTEMS

Single-Unit Design. Here, all the basic components (such as the microprocessor and RAM storage) are mounted on one large printed-circuit board. This type can be further subdivided according to the type of microprocessor used. MOS-technology designed 6502 microprocessor unit is used in Atari, Commodore, and Apple computers. Except for the Radio Shack line, Z-80 microprocessor use is restricted mainly to small business systems.

Fully Assembled Mother Board Units. The mother board system is a design in which the individual system functions, such as CPU and memory, are divided into individual plug-in boards (Fig. 5-1). Each of the individual boards plugs into the mother board that carries the interconnections (called the *data bus*). There are, basically, two different data bus interconnection systems. The IEEE S-100 bus systems generally use the Intel 8080 or Zilog Z-80 microprocessor. The **SS-50** bus systems generally use the Motorola designed 6800/6809 microprocessors.

Of course, technologies overlap. Hence, some CPU 6800 cards are made for the S-100 bus, and some Z-80 cards for the SS-50 bus.

To repeat, you can acquire your home-computer system either by buying individual components and building it yourself, or by purchasing an assembled system. Building up a system one piece at a time can, in the long run, cost more, but there's both fun and extra satisfaction in establishing your own system parameters. Careful study of the basic system and components is required in order to get compatible systems, of course: an S-100 bus doesn't go with a SS-50 bus, for example.

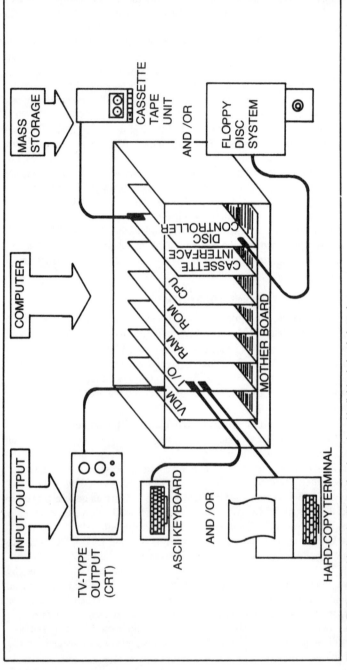

Fig. 5-1. Fully assembled unit with mother board and individual plug-in boards.

Whichever route you decide to take, keep one thing in mind: Your end purpose. Never stop asking, What do I want the computer for? What do I want it to do? That's the important thing: what the device can do for *you*.

SOFTWARE

There are two fundamental and closely related considerations of great concern to the home computerist: software and memory. The software selected will determine the size of the memory and peripheral capabilities. Obviously, it doesn't make much sense to invest in a computer with the capability of a 40-character line if you want to do word processing, and the word-processing software requires an 80-character line. Such computer publications as *Personal Computing, On Computing,* and *Byte* carry pages and pages of information on software suppliers. The following suppliers offer catalogs worth sending for. (There are others, but try these for starters.)

● Micro Computer Software (256 South Robertson Boulevard, Suite 2156, Beverly Hills, CA 90211) offers *Typing Without Errors, The Teacher Plus, Tax Planning, Personal Text Processor,* and others.

● GRT Corporation (1286 Lawrence Station Road, Sunnyvale, CA 94086) offers three catalogs of software (Fig. 5-2).

Fig. 5-2. Sample software programs.
(Courtesy, GRT Corporation.)

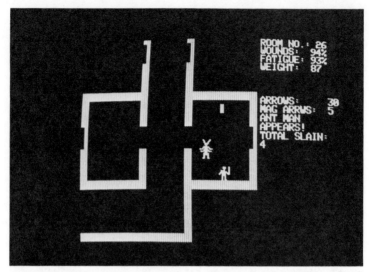

Fig. 5-3. Sample screen image of game software, "The Datastones of Ryn." (Courtesy, Automated Simulations Inc.)

● The Bottom Shelf Company (P.O. Box 49104, Atlanta, GA 30359) offers a large number of catalogs, with so many software programs that a listing here is impossible.

● High Sierra Software (5541 Highway 50 East, Suite 2A, Carson City, NV 89701) offers software programs especially geared to the kitchen, telephone, alarm, timer, home inventory, home payables, home checkbook, interest payments/calculations, real estate, recipes, insurance, computer art, and others.

● Micro-Ed Inc. (P.O. Box 24156, Minneapolis, MN 55424) has programs for grammar use, arithmetic and advanced math, music, reading, reference skills, spelling, vocabulary, and others.

● Automated Simulations Inc. (1988 Leghorn Street, Mountain View, CA 94043) boasts a variety of games, such as The "Treasures of Apshai," "Rescue at Rigel," "Morloc's Tower," and "The Datasontes of Ryn" (Fig. 5-3).

Most software programs are designed for a particular computer system or systems and can only be used with the system(s) indicated. Look for such qualifiers as "for Apple and TRS-80 computers only."

Computer suppliers also have a number of software programs available to go with their systems. (They're smart enough not to let other vendors control the rich software market!) For example, Fig. 5-4 shows Radio Shack's software package for personal stock portfolio management.

While your initial software selection won't be the critical factor in your decision about which personal/home computer system to buy, it will help to point the way toward the type of computer you ultimately decide upon.

WHAT'S YOUR COMPUTER KNOWHOW RATING?

There's another factor to consider before you buy a home computer: your own experience and qualifications as a computer user. Are you a novice? An intermediate user? An advanced professional? Ask yourself this important question, and answer it honestly.

By novice, of course, I mean someone who has just become interested in computers. An intermediate-class user is one who has perhaps worked with computers before, but only to the extent of having run off-the-shelf applications programs, either through a cassette or floppy disc. You're an advanced user if you've done your own programming; are experienced in other languages besides BASIC; or have stored programs in hard-disc drives. You should make yourself a list like that shown in Fig. 5-5.

Recent developments in the market place have created an almost automatic segmenting of personal/home computers according to price and performance. Apple, Atari, and Radio Shack computers, for example, are 8-bit up based systems costing less than $5,000. At the same time, such new entrants in the marketplace as IBM, Xerox, DEC, and DG are selling 16-bit up systems for $5,000 to $15,000.

WHERE TO BUY YOUR COMPUTER

There are three outlets for home computers. Computer stores, special retail outlets either independent or part of a franchise operation, often have sales personnel with considerable computer knowledge. They'll help you

Fig. 5-4. Stockpak software system lets you manage your own stock portfolio. (Courtesy, Radio Shack.)

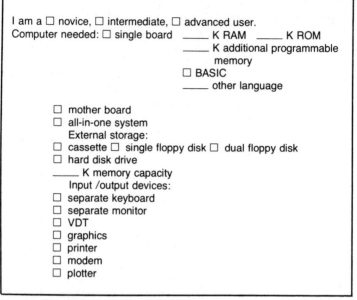

I am a ☐ novice, ☐ intermediate, ☐ advanced user.
Computer needed: ☐ single board ＿＿ K RAM ＿＿ K ROM
＿＿ K additional programmable
memory
☐ BASIC
＿＿ other language

☐ mother board
☐ all-in-one system
External storage:
☐ cassette ☐ single floppy disk ☐ dual floppy disk
☐ hard disk drive
＿＿ K memory capacity
Input /output devices:
☐ separate keyboard
☐ separate monitor
☐ VDT
☐ graphics
☐ printer
☐ modem
☐ plotter

Fig. 5-5. Pre-purchase computer checklist.

assemble the necessary configuration of hardware, based on your software requirements.

Department stores such as Sears, J.C. Penney, and Montgomery Ward, are now selling personal/home computers, including private-label versions of some brands.

Finally, a number of manufacturers have opened their own retail computer outlets.

You can also buy used computer equipment, of course: you'll find listings in most of the computer-oriented publications. Most used-equipment dealers publish their own catalogs, and maintain fairly extensive mailing lists. A postcard will probably get you any dealer's latest used-equipment catalog, and you'll find that these dealers are eager to do business. You have to watch warranty statements, of course, and be careful that any equipment you buy is not too old, since getting parts for older hardware can present a problem.

HOME COMPUTER COMMUNICATIONS

One interesting aspect of owning your own computer is the possibility of communicating over *network*—provided you have the right system to do so. *Networking* is the linking together of individuals and information. There are two major networks for consumer-oriented communications systems, both of them based on telephone lines (and both of them mentioned earlier in these pages): The Source (Source Telecomputing Corporation, 1616 Anderson Road, McLean, VA 22102) and CompuServe (5000 Arlington Center Boulevard, Columbus, OH 43220).

The Source is a telecomputing network that gives you access to literally thousands of programs and data bases, including the ability to communicate with other users, both interactively and through electronic mail. You can tap into the UPI newswire that provides you information broken into such categories as general, business, features, and sports, at the regional, national, or international level. Through The Source you can also extract information from *The New York Times* Consumer Data Base, which offers thousands of capsulized articles, covering everything from abortion to white-collar crime. More than 120 research categories are available, with an average of 30 to 40 stories per category. All of this information is stored until it is six days old, after which it's purged from the data base. You may also run programs that deal with taxes or the stock market.

The most exciting part for most people is that you can communicate with other Source subscribers. After you've paid your initial hookup fee, you can turn on your computer, turn on your modem, pick up the phone, and dial the nearest number in the Telenet Telephone Access list, you then place the phone handset on the modem and conduct a cryptic conversation with whoever is at the other end.

There are a number of charges connected with the use of The Source, of course, including a minimum monthly charge for storage of information obtained from the data base and a per-hour charge for use of the phone line. There are phone numbers for 300 cities, so you don't have to worry about paying for long-distance phone calls. A monthly publication, *Sourceworld*, keeps you up to date with new developments and general news about the service.

Also, when you sign up you receive a complete user's package, consisting of a *User's Guide & Master Index*, account number, password, and list of available software programs.

CompuServe offers basically the same kind of capabilities as The Source, is available through all Radio Shack dealers. The initial hookup fee is much less than that for The Source, while their minimum charges and phone charges vary.

CompuServe has 23 metropolitan cities on-line, plus more than 200 smaller cities involved through the Tymnet professional time-sharing organization.

MISCELLANEOUS COMPUTER-AIDED DEVICES

Other devices, although not full-fledged home computers, use computer technology and provide basic computer experience in their use.

Milton Bradley Big Trak

You and your family may have been using computers for some time, without ever knowing it. If, for example, you bought your child the Milton

Bradley Big Trak, he or she has been programming without being aware of it as he plays with his toy. The Big Trak (Fig. 5-6) is sold with a very simple program already placed (preprogrammed) in its memory (RAM). You child can program up to 16 different steps by entering instructions into the keyboard, exactly as you'd do with the keyboard of a "big" computer.

For example, when you press CLR, ⬆ 2, ⬇ 2, and GO in succession, the toy will move forward a distance two times its length, and then backwards a distance two times its length. The toy can make left or right turns, fire its gun at a certain moment, hold in position for a time, and repeat certain actions—all of them programmed. You can also clear the last instruction if you change your mind about the last program step. This prevents you from completely reprogramming the sequences in case of an error, in much the way a personal/home computer would handle it.

Tiger Electronics K-2-8

Another toy that actually *looks* like a computer is Tiger Electronics' "K-2-8" Talking Learning Computer (Fig. 5-7). This machine offers a combination of three primary educational functions—mathematics, spelling, and reading readiness—in one compact unit. With a 1500-word vocabulary and 15 usable modes, the computer introduces children to new facets of the English language, including vocabulary expansion and spelling; geography and history; mathematics and problem solving; social studies; and science.

Fig. 5-6. Big Trak computer-controlled toy. (Courtesy, Milton Bradley Co.)

Fig. 5-7. K-2-8 Talking Learning Computer. (Courtesy, Tiger Electronics.)

The most interesting aspect from our point of view is that in the course of using the machine, certain simple programming steps have to be taken, thus introducing the child to the use of computers. For example certain modes have to be selected, such as problem format and level of difficulty; true or false; multiple choice; yes or no; and fill in the blank. The K-2-8 computer uses modules as its software. A 56-key keyboard and a vacuum fluorescent display are hardware components that let the child—and you too!—get acquainted with "computerism." At this time no instruction book is available.

Entex Industries MAC

Another computer of interest is the MAC minicomputer from Entex Industries. This battery-operated unit (Fig. 5-8) is a 4-K microcomputer with numeric keyboard, a simulated CRT with 16-LED matrix display, and an 8-digit readout that includes an illuminated slide reader.

The computer has been programmed to let you perform such calculator functions as addition, subtraction, multiplication, and division of numbers up to 8 digits. You can also listen to songs that you've entered into the computer's memory, and play such games as tic-tac-toe, slot machine, tactics, concentration, and world time. You'll learn simple programming as you devise games of your own, using the calculator. A small speaker reproduces sounds and music.

The display matrix consists of 16 lights (Fig. 5-9) composed of four rows and four columns, while the keyboard (Fig. 5-10) can be used in four

Fig. 5-8. MAC minicomputer. (Courtesy, Entex Industries.)

different modes as follows: *music mode,* (Fig. 5-11); *calculator mode* (Fig. 5-12); *game mode* (Fig. 5-13); and *programming mode* (Fig. 5-14)—each with its distinctive light pattern on the display panel.

In the musical mode you can listen to a song that's been permanently stored in the computer's memory, plus record and play back songs you've stored in the memory. Using the musical keyboard, you can stretch up to two octaves. The computer can't handle chords (two or more notes played at the same time), but it is able to play sharps and flats—the black keys on a piano. The frequencies (pitches of sound) of the notes that the computer can play are given in Table 5-1, and of sharps and flats in Table 5-2.

In the calculator mode, you can execute a number of calculations, such as multiplying and dividing two negative numbers, exponential calculations, and basic math.

Fig. 5-9. Matrix display panel of MAC minicomputer. (Courtesy, Entex Industries.)

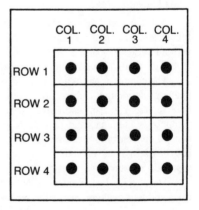

Games you can play include being the first to reach 21, determining birthdays, and guessing a number closest to the cubic power of a base number. Also in the game mode, the computer will play five preprogrammed games stored in its memory: *Tic-tac-toe*, in which the object is to be the first player to light up three entries in a row, vertically, horizontally, or diagonally; *tactics*, in which the idea is to force your opponent to switch off the last light in the light matrix; *concentration*, which involves scoring as many points as possible by occupying entries in a 4 × 4 display matrix; *world time*, to whose object is to find out the correct local time of any city listed in the world time-zone chart; and *slot machine*, where the objective is to score as many points as possible by lining up lights in any one column of the display matrix.

One, interesting and fascinating aspect of this computer is the feel you get for programming when you set the computer in the programming mode. Although it's not otherwise similar to BASIC programming, it has the same practical format of step-by-step instructions. Those who have never entered a program into a computer will get a good feel for how this is accomplished.

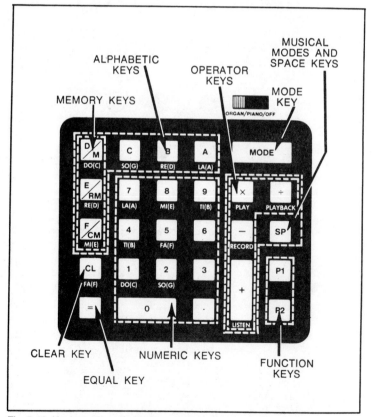

Fig. 5-10. Keyboard layout of MAC minicomputer. (Courtesy, Entex Industries.)

113

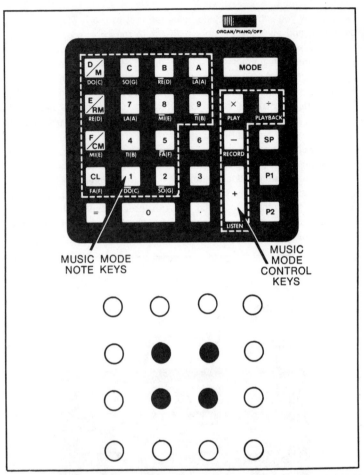

Fig. 5-11. Keys used in music mode and accompanying LED light pattern in MAC computer. (Courtesy, Entex Industries.)

There are 11 different input codes, consisting of 53 instructions. A sample follows:

1-1 through 1-8 Specify light to turn ON
1-9   Specify all lights to turn ON
2-1 through 2-8 Specify all lights to turn ON
2-9   Specify all lights to turn OFF
3-1   Turn on specified lights
4-1 through 4-4 Pause for 0.1 to 1.0 second
5-1 through 5-7 Specify note to play DO-TI
6-1 through 6-7 Specify note to play DO-TI
7-1 through 7-7 Specify duration of notes [naturals]

8-1 through 8-7	Specify duration of notes [sharps]
9-1	Produce note
9-9	End of program

Athena 2000 Singer Sewing Machine

If you're using a Singer Athena 2000 sewing machine to do your home sewing, you're using a computer with RAM and ROM memory and I/O devices—all based on the same computer principles described in earlier chapters.

You simply turn a dial that displays one of the LED stitch patterns above one of the six touch-sensitive selector keys. After you've selected the desired pattern, the microprocessor searches for the pattern within its ROM memory and outputs the pattern's digital codes (Fig. 5-15). Pattern

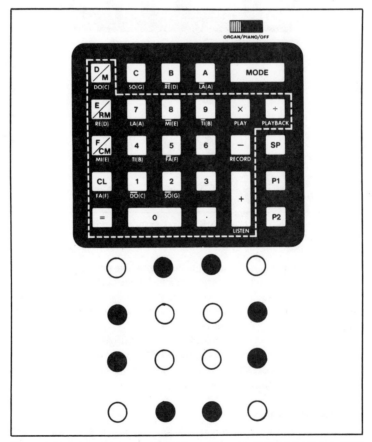

Fig. 5-12. Keys for calculator mode and accompanying LED light pattern in MAC computer. (Courtesy, Entex Industries.)

115

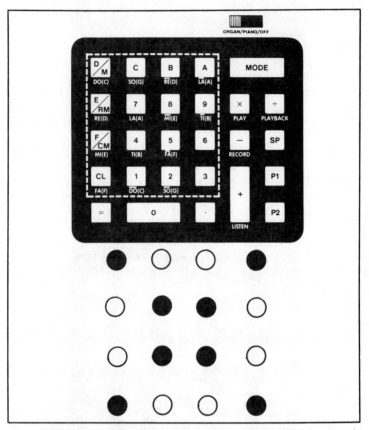

Fig. 5-13. Keys to be used in game mode and accompanying LED light pattern in MAC computer. (Courtesy, Entex Industries.)

control is separated into lateral commands for needle position, and forward and backward commands for fabric position. Besides being responsible for the pattern search, the microprocessor is also responsible for directing the motions of two linear servomotors that control the needle and fabric positions, respectively, as read out of the ROM.

When you look at the available stitch patterns (Fig. 5-16) you'll see that a lot of memory has to be stored - 5 kB in ROM. Yet the computer is capable of *doubling* the length of the programmed stitch, as well as reversing the direction of the stitch to provide a mirror image of any pattern!

Computer-Controlled Telephones

Are you familiar with the telephone that has, besides the normal keypad, a number of "extra" buttons? Well, this kind of computer-controlled telephone has the capability of storing frequently dialed numbers in memory,

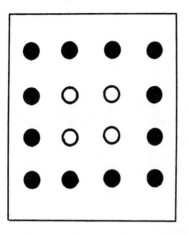

Fig. 5-14. Programming mode light pattern in MAC computer. (Courtesy, Entex Industries.)

performing automatic dialing for you (while you leave the handset on the hook), and even automatically redialing a busy number!

Most such telephones use computer chips—integrated circuits. They utilize low-power CMOS circuitry that allows operation from low-power telephone lines. Repertory dialer chips (Fig. 5-17) are presently used in many automatic dialing systems. The computer accepts inputs from a keypad (analogous to the keyboard of your home computer) and stores the phone numbers entered in a separate memory chip. This computer chip can automatically redial stored numbers, and can display the number being dialed. The computer also controls a tone generator or dial pulse generator to synthesize with the standard telephone dial tone or dual-tone multifrequency signals.

Table 5-1. Frequencies of Notes Computer Can Play in MAC (Musical Mode)

Tone	Musical Note	Approximate Output Frequency (in Hz)
Do	C^1	263
Re	D^1	293
Mi	E^1	326
Fa	F^1	347
So	G^1	388
La	A^1	440
Ti	B^1	486
Do	C^2	520
Re	D^2	586
Mi	E^2	652
Fa	F^2	694
So	G^2	776
La	A^2	880
Ti	B^2	972

Tone	Output Frequency (in Hz)
C#^{1} (or D b^1)	276
D#^{1} (or E b^1)	309
F#^{1} (or G b^1)	367
G#^{1} (or A b^1)	414
A#^{1} (or B b^1)	463
C#^{2} (or D b^2)	553
D#^{2} (or E b^2)	619
F#^{2} (or G b^2)	736
G#^{2} (or A b^2)	828
A#^{2} (or B b^2)	926

Table 5-2. Frequencies of Notes (Sharps and Flats) the Computer Can Play, MAC (Musical Mode)

Automobile Computer-Command Controls

Are you driving a 1981 Chrysler Imperial by any chance? If you are, you're already deeper into computers than you may have realized. The instrument panel of this automobile uses vacuum-fluorescent readouts to display digitally the readings of the odometer, speedometer, gear selector, and fuel indicator. In addition, a special safety-control panel signals brake problems; a door that's ajar; such engine parameters as oil pressure, coolant temperature, and system voltage; burned out bulbs; and computer malfunctions.

The system uses two microprocessors (Fig. 5-18) to accumulate sensor data and to compute and display function values. It stores odometer readings in its memory.

All 1981 GM cars employ a CCC: computer-command control. In this system, an electronic module (Fig. 5-19) acts as the system's computer, continuously monitoring coolant temperature, engine speed, intake manifold pressure, throttle position, and exhaust gas-oxygen content. This computer system combines adaptive software with a continuously powered memory, designed around an 8-bit 6802 microprocessor.

The four other integrated circuits are for control logic, memory, analog-to-digital conversion, and a power-conditioning board. The microprocessor is a 40-pin device that adds 10 instructions to the standard 6800 instruction set, including an 8-bit multiplication and double-precision addition, subtraction, stacking, and accumulator instructions. The engine-control unit (Fig. 5-20) is a microprogrammed controller, processing both input and output signals. Finally, the memory combination holds the software of 4K bytes of ROM and 128 bytes of RAM.

COMPUTERIZED HOMES

If automobiles with their complicated workings can be computer-controlled, why can't we build the same ideas into our homes? Well, all computer connections are accomplished through wiring systems, and it's

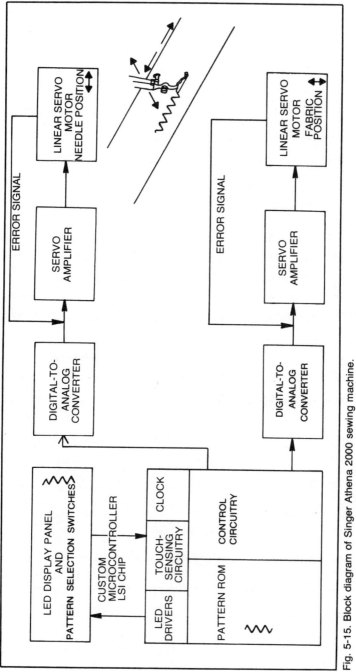

Fig. 5-15. Block diagram of Singer Athena 2000 sewing machine.

119

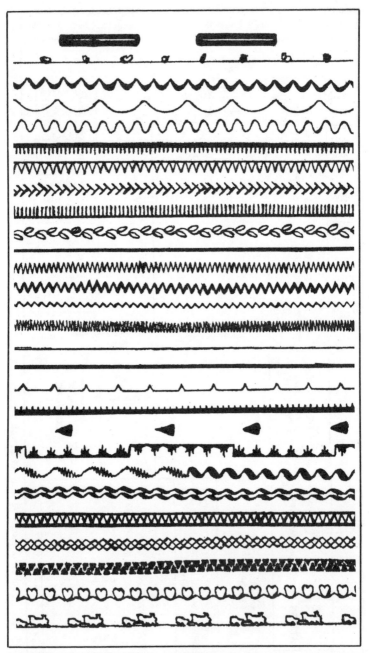

Fig. 5-16. A few stitching patterns of computer-controlled Singer Athena 2000 sewing machine. (Courtesy, Singer Sewing Machine Co.)

relatively easy to wire a computer system into an automobile, because of its compactness. Wiring a home is much more complex: there are different codes to contend with, for one thing, and the installation is cumbersome and complex, for another.

However, you can have a home where a computer takes complete control of environmental and other household functions: the Semiconductor Group of Motorola did just that. The Ahwatukee House they built in Phoenix, Arizona, has a complete home-management computer system, organized to control five basic areas: information, security, environment, electrical-load switching, and energy management. Each of five areas of the house—living room, kitchen, master bedroom, laundry room and equipment room—has its own microcomputer, each with its own functions (Fig. 5-21).

For example, the kitchen microcomputer has wall-switch inputs and relay-load outputs, so it must perform the electrical load- and switch-

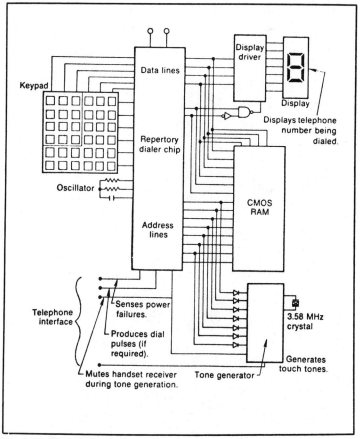

Fig. 5-17. Block diagram of repertory dialer.

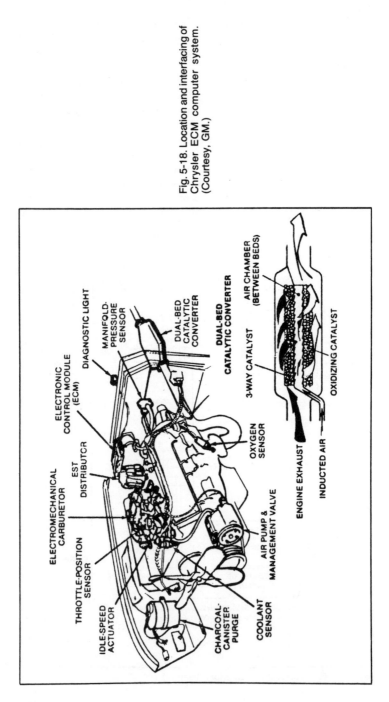

Fig. 5-18. Location and interfacing of Chrysler ECM computer system. (Courtesy, GM.)

DIAGNOSTIC LIGHT

MANIFOLD-PRESSURE SENSOR

ELECTRONIC CONTROL MODULE (ECM)

DUAL-BED CATALYTIC CONVERTER

ELECTROMECHANICAL CARBURETOR

EST DISTRIBUTOR

THROTTLE-POSITION SENSOR

IDLE-SPEED ACTUATOR

CHARCOAL-CANISTER PURGE

COOLANT SENSOR

AIR PUMP & MANAGEMENT VALVE

OXYGEN SENSOR

DUAL-BED CATALYTIC CONVERTER

AIR CHAMBER (BETWEEN BEDS)

3-WAY CATALYST

OXIDIZING CATALYST

ENGINE EXHAUST

INDUCTED AIR

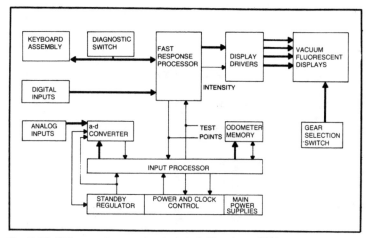

Fig. 5-19. GM computer command control. (Courtesy, GM.)

manager functions. The information storage and retrieval function goes with the television set and keyboard. One of the sitting-room microcomputers services the equipment room located outside: its environmental function takes analog inputs from indoor and outdoor temperature and humidity sensors, and controls relay loads. (The relay loads require the load-manager function.)

The electrical load-switching capability conserves energy by allowing the computers to control lights, wall outlets, and electrical equipment. Lights can be programmed by the homeowner to turn on and off at various times during the day or night, while motion detectors will light on or off when someone enters or leaves the room.

The computer determines whether one of the three zones in the house requires heating or cooling. When, for example, one zone in the house is too hot, the computer automatically opens certain doors or windows.

Security control covers both intrusion and fire; electronic keypads are used on all doors instead of regular keys. Special codes allow access to the homeowner, while service personnel are restricted to an access code that's valid only during specific hours of the day.

The computers also have voice capability: when you enter the door—after having recited the proper access code—the computer will greet you by name. (Similarly, the computer can warn the homeowner when an illegal intrusion occurs.)

The computers are interconnected through a loop of five network nodes. An executive program resident in each computer organizes the system processes: disc, display, load manager, switch manager, security, energy management, environmental, time and printer—for each of the five nodes. (See Fig. 5-22). Although each computer has several resident processes, some of which are duplicated among the computers, no computer

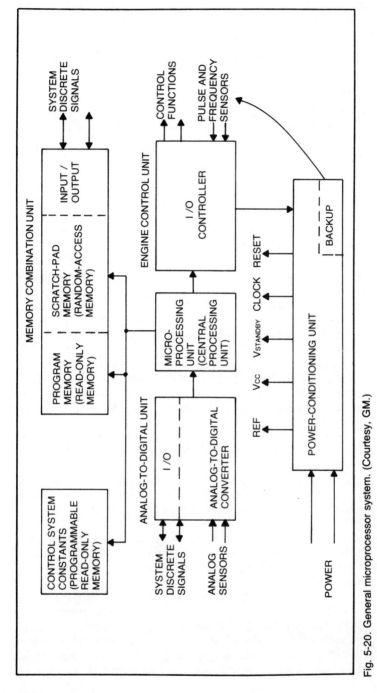

Fig. 5-20. General microprocessor system. (Courtesy, GM.)

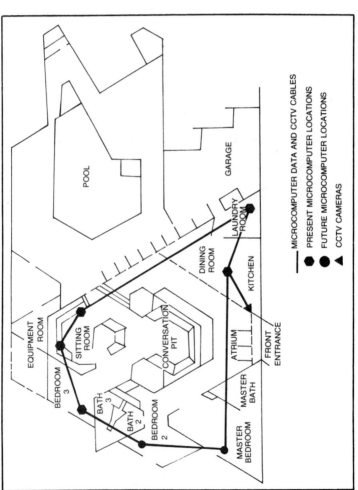

Fig. 5-21. Location of computers throughout house (see text).

125

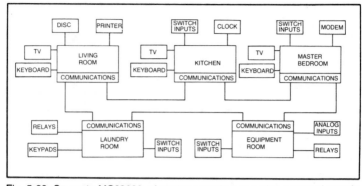

Fig. 5-22. Separate MC68000 microprocessor-based nodes communicate via an intelligent communications processor and data-link controller.

contains all processes; therefore, failure of one computer won't necessarily cause all processes to go down.

Battery backup is provided in case of power failure. The printer produces a hard copy of any text displayed on the TV screens, permitting the printing of material or information that might be needed away from the house. One company—Motorola—is working hard on modifying the system in such a way that any future installations can be accomplished and handled by the homeowner.

There's no need, however, to wait for the fully computerized house. Right now, you can have—not a computer-controlled home, exactly but the means to provide the family with the control of many household functions by and through a computer.

Part 2
State of the Art

Chapter 6
Computers:
What's Available

This final chapter describes some of the personal/home computers presently available in the marketplace. Some systems are discussed extensively, others just mentioned briefly. To describe and discuss every computer on the market would be impossible within the framework of this book.

APF IMAGINATION MACHINE

The core unit of the APF Imagination Machine is a straightforward video game, complete with a pair of multifunction hand controllers (Fig. 6-1). Each controller features four-way game paddles, a 12-key calculator-style pad, and a "fire" button for some video games (Fig. 6-2). The controllers are permanently wired to the console.

Connecting the console to any black-and-white or color television set is simple. If the rear of your set looks like Fig. 6-3, then disconnect the flat wire from the set and connect it to the APF switch box at the "300 ohm" location. Then connect the flat wire from the switch box to the VHF terminals of your television set.

If the rear of your set looks like Fig. 6-4, then move the slider to make the connection between screws; disconnect the cable from your television set and plug it into the APF switch box at the "75 ohm" location; and connect the flat wire of the switch box to the VHF terminals of your set.

In the third possibility, if your television rear panel looks like Fig. 6-5, then disconnect the cable from your set and plug it into the switch box at the 75 ohm location; connect your set's short, loose-hanging wire to the connector next to it on the set, and connect the flat wire of the switch box to the VHF terminals of your set. Whichever connection you make, you're ready now to use the various game cartridges to play video games on your television set.

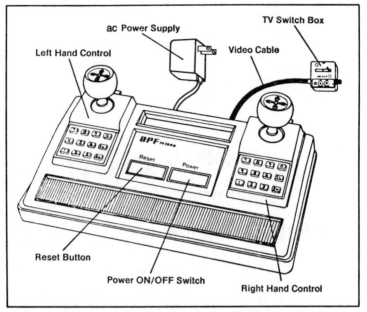

Fig. 6-1. MP-1000 Imagination Machine console. (Courtesy, APF Electronics.)

This Model MP-1000 console can be nestled into a computer module MP-10 (Fig. 6-6), a computer system with full typewriter-style keyboard, dual-track cassette recorder, and built-in speaker. Nestled together, the two systems form one personal computer (Fig. 6-7).

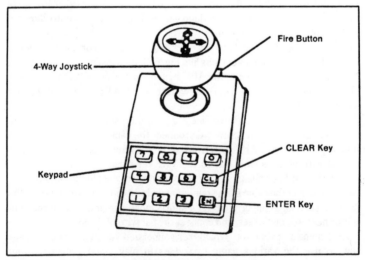

Fig. 6-2. Hand controller of MP-1000 Imagination Machine.

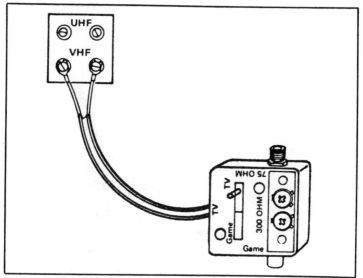

Fig. 6-3. Connecting switch box to TV set (version 1).

An expansion interface, with four universally adaptable ports, easily plugs into the computer system to perform different functions. For example:

● One RS-232 interface cartridge allows you to connect to the system most RS-232 serial devices.

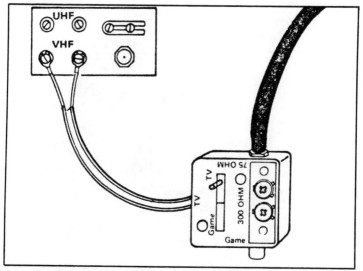

Fig. 6-4. Connecting switch box to TV set (version 2).

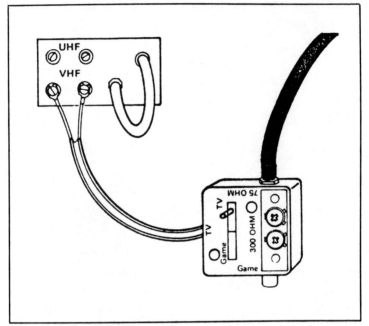

Fig. 6-5. Connecting switch box to TV set (version 3).

Fig. 6-6. Computer console MP-10 of Imagination Machine. (Courtesy, APF Electronics.)

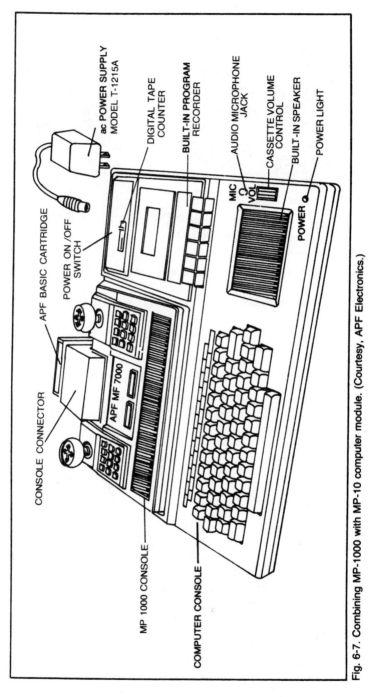

Fig. 6-7. Combining MP-1000 with MP-10 computer module. (Courtesy, APF Electronics.)

- ac POWER SUPPLY MODEL T-1215A
- DIGITAL TAPE COUNTER
- **BUILT-IN PROGRAM** RECORDER
- AUDIO MICROPHONE JACK
- CASSETTE VOLUME CONTROL
- BUILT-IN SPEAKER
- POWER LIGHT
- APF BASIC CARTRIDGE
- POWER ON/OFF SWITCH
- CONSOLE CONNECTOR
- MP 1000 CONSOLE
- COMPUTER CONSOLE

MIC
VOL
POWER

APF MF 7000

Fig. 6-8. APF Imagination Machine. (Courtesy, APF Electronics.)

● A mini-floppy interface cartridge allows you to drive two standard 5-¼ floppy-disc drives.

● A parallel interface cartridge allows you to connect most parallel devices to the system.

● An 8K RAM cartridge will increase your memory storage by an additional 8K, and a 16K RAM cartridge by twice that amount.

Two mini-floppy disc drives, available as optional peripherals, each have a capacity of 72K bytes per single-sided disc. Figure 6-8 shows the two modules together, and Fig. 6-9 shows the expandable system. Using the RS-232 interface cartridge, you can connect a model (Fig. 6-10) to the system, which allows you to obtain information from various data bases such as (the Source and CompuServe) and to communicate with other computer users.

The Imagination Machine contains a machine language reference mode that you can use to create, display, change, and execute machine-language programs. However, you must be able to write programs in 6800 machine language. You must also have a working knowledge of hexadecimal notation.

Included with the Imagination Machine is a BASIC cartridge that has to be inserted in the rear of the computer console (Fig. 6-11). This cartridge lets you work with that computer language, or—if you're interested in learning BASIC—APF has a program called BASIC Tutor. An instruction manual and 22 programs on cassette tapes help guide you through the Tutor program, where you'll learn about commands, program statements, arithmetic functions, and much more. You can also play music with the program, and create your own graphics in eight colors.

The built-in cassette recorder/player allows you to run various pro-

Fig. 6-9. Expandable system of Imagination Machine — MPII with expansion unit and interface and memory cartridges. (Courtesy, APF Electronics.)

grams, as well as save data and use regular audio recording with digital recording. The cassette is a dual-track tape unit, so you can record your voice or music on the same tape as your computer program.

This is an interesting machine, especially for those who are just starting to work with computers.

APPLE COMPUTER

When the Apple Computer Company introduced the Apple I computer, it created a sensation. And no wonder: here at last was a single-board computer that sold for a very low price.

Fig. 6-10. APF modem for communications with time-sharing organizations and other computers. (Courtesy, APF Electronics.)

135

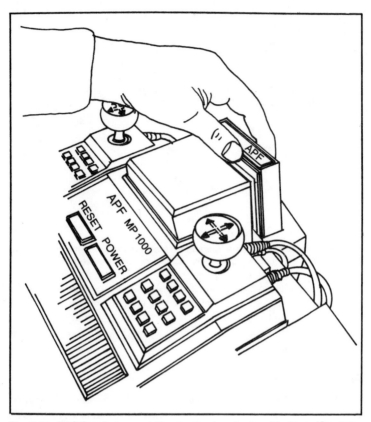

Fig. 6-11. BASIC software cartridge for the Imagination Machine. (Courtesy, APF Electronics.)

Within a year the company introduced the Apple II, a powerful computer (at the time) that needed only to be plugged in and attached to video to make it work. However, the machine had BASIC Integer as its operating system and numerical calculations couldn't be done with this type of system software. So, Apple II+ was introduced with Apple BASIC Microsoft, or APPLESOFT, as the system software. With the recently introduced Apple III, the company now has three computers on the market.

Apple II and II+

These machines (Fig. 6-12) have a single-board 6502 computer in an injection-molded plastic case with a built-in keyboard. They are capable of holding 64K of RAM and 16K of ROM. The basic 16K RAM can be increased through cartridge increments, there are slots in the back of the units that accept the various boards for memory expansion.

The Apple II doesn't come with a VDT, and you must furnish your own television set or monitor to accept the alphanumeric text and color graphics. However, there are several additional peripherals and accessories you can use with Apple II:

Floppy-Disc Drives. Two disc drives interface by using a board placed in one of the sockets in the rear of the unit.

Graphics Tablet. This tablet and its pen connect to the table interface board that plugs into one of the peripheral sockets of the system. After installing this board, you use the graphics tablet software disc with the floppy-disc drive. Command boxes across the top front of the tablet offer 22 separate functions, making it possible for you to switch modes simply by pressing the pen to the desired command box. If you want to draw a landscape, for example, you press the DRAW command box and then the PEN COLOR box. A color options menu will appear on the screen. You then move the pen lightly across the tablet, and an indicator will drift across the screen at the same time, signaling that the pen is in contact with the tablet. You continue to move the pen until the indicator comes to rest on the color block you want. Pressing down on the tablet at this time will make the menu disappear, and you're ready for the first stroke in your chosen color.

When you want to change to another color you simply press PEN COLOR command again and repeat the selection process. An error can easily be corrected by selecting the color you want and drawing over the mistake. In the maximum drawing space of 11 × 10 inches, you can do block diagrams, architectural renderings, mechanical shapes, fine art—just about anything you want to draw.

Fig. 6-12. Apple II Computer with video monitor, two floppy-disc drives, and printer. (Courtesy, Apple Computer Co.)

There are nine tablet modes, such as BKGND COLOR, which set the entire screen to the chosen color; six pen modes, such as DRAW, which draws lines; and five command modes.

Thermal Printer. The Apple Silentype printer interfaces with the computer by means of an interface board that fits in one of the sockets in the rear of the machine. The unit prints upper and lowercase characters with a speed of up to 40 characters per second, 80 characters per line. High-resolution graphics are printed at 60 dots per inch. The printer prints clear, readable copy on white heat-sensitive paper.

Daisy-Wheel Printer. The Qume Sprint 5 printer is a fully formed character impact printer that operates at a speed of 45 characters per second. It also interfaces with the computer by means of an interface board.

Apple Joystick. This single joystick plugs into the game's I/O socket, offering you the opportunity to play certain games more effectively and avoiding more flexibility in applications requiring advanced hand input capabilities.

Interface Cards. The *Serial Interface Card* allows the computer to interface (that is, exchange data) with other computers, printers, and accessories in serial format one bit at a time. *Communications Interface Card* lets you connect your computer to modems, CRT terminals, and other devices employing a bidirectional, serial interface. *Parallel Interface Card* gives your computer the capability to generate reports, listings, letters, and the like, using parallel interfaced printers.

Apple Computer Peripherals

In addition, many vendors advertise extensively in computer publications, offering software, peripherals, and accessories for the Apple Computers. One such company is Emtrol Systems Inc., which offers the Lynx telephone linkage system, a hardwired modem. (See Fig. 6-13.) These companies make the installation of peripherals very easy. The Lynx comes with all necessary attaching cables; by simply plugging the unit in with the various connectors (Fig. 6-14) the device becomes immediately operable.

Many of these accessories expand the capabilities of the original computer. For example, the Apple II has a 40 columns × 24 lines of text capability. Videx Company offers a Videoterm that increases the capacity of the screen to 24 × 80 in a 7 × 9 matrix, or 18 × 80 in a 7 × 12 matrix.

Scott Instruments provides the VET/2, a speech-recognition device consisting of a microphone, a hardware preprocessor with an Apple interface board, and software (which is designed to reside in Apple's 48K RAM). The preprocessor analyzes an acoustic signal within a 300-Hz to 4,000-Hz frequency range. Analysis consists of breaking the frequency range into two regions—300-1000 Hz and 1000-4000 Hz—taking zero-crossing measures in both regions, and extracting the amplitude envelope of the two regions. The four resulting analog data lines are then converted into digital form at the request of the computer.

Fig. 6-13. Hard-wired modem for use with the Apple II computer. (Courtesy, Emtrol Systems Inc.)

There's a direct keyboard link that allows you to choose keyboard input or voice input at any time. When you want to run word-processor programs with voice input, you simply call the training routine; type the character, word, or phrase you want to enter on the keyboard; say the word five times; and return to the program. Thereafter, when that word is spoken, the matching function is automatically performed by the computer. Figure 6-15 shows the device located on top of the computer.

The reason you have to say the word five times is that the device is speaker-dependent—that is, it must be trained for your voice. It recognizes isolated utterances of up to 1.5 sec. duration and allows an active vocabulary of 40 entries.)

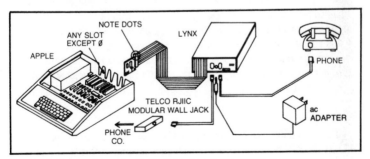

Fig. 6-14. Connecting a hard-wired modem to the Apple II computer.

Fig. 6-15. VET/2 speech-recognition unit situated on top of an Apple II computer. (Courtesy, Scott Instruments Co.)

ALF Products Inc. supplies a number of music synthesizer boards you can use to play "computer music" through your Apple Computer. By plugging the boards into the appropriate slots of the computer and attaching your hi-fi and speaker system, you can use the supplied software either to enter music from a music sheet (or your own compositions!) in the computer, or to record and store music from "programmed song albums"—music stored on floppy discs or cassettes.

The Apple III

This is a 6502-based computer that can address up to 512K bytes of RAM, with 128K bytes being the regular supplied unit. A floppy-disc drive, a RS-232 serial interface, a dual joystick interface, and external sound built into the unit. The Apple III has four expansion slots, similar to the ones in the

Apple II; an alphanumeric keyboard is also part of the system. The video screen supports a 40- or 80-column by 24 line text display with user-definable characters and several high-resolution graphics modes. Figure 6-16 illustrates the Apple III.

As many as four different peripheral cards can be used at one time to supplement the unit's built-in peripheral interfaces. Also, thermal printer or daisy-wheel printer and modem can be attached to the system, and a variety of software is available for the Apple III.

ASTROVISION BALLY ARCADE

The basic unit in this system is a video game (top of Fig. 6-17). This system—which contains three microprocessors—comes with three built-in games, built-in calculator, keypad, two eight-way hand controls, cassette program storage I/O, and light pen connector. Hand controls, or joysticks, allow you to create interactive games with extensive motion. Tunes and realistic sound effects are created with the three-channel music synthesizer and sound-effects generator.

The three processors include a Z-80 CPU, operating at 1.8 MHz; a video processor that handles all color manipulation and animation speeds; and an I/O processor that handles the joystick and keypad inputs and creates the sound effects. Three separate sound synthesizers work with both AM and FM noise and a frequency range of 2 Hz to 100 kHz.

The Arcade can be expanded in either of two ways: One way is with a plug-in cartridge with a built-in cassette tape interface that converts the

Fig. 6-16. Apple III Computer. (Courtesy, The Apple Computer Co.)

Fig. 6-17. Bally Arcade Video Game/Computer system from Astrovision. (Courtesy, Astrovision.)

basic unit into a personal/home computer you can program yourself. A library of BASIC software on cassette can teach you programming techniques. You can program colors, shapes, music, and sound effects, selecting from 256 possible combinations by picking each of the two colors on the screen (your own monitor or television set). The built-in music system converts the keypad into a three-octave music keyboard, including sharps and flats. The cassette interface, finally, lets you store and save programs on a cassette recorder.

The other method uses a Zgrass keyboard that plugs into the Arcade to give you a full typewriter alphanumeric keyboard. You also get an additional 32K RAM and 24K ROM.

Expansion modules offer you the capability of adding such peripherals as a floppy-disc expansion, light pen, drawing tablet, and RS-232 modem printer. This keyboard expansion allows you to create more complex graphs, video art, and other visual effects. Plug-in cartridges with up to 16K ROM can be used to add additional languages and turnkey graphic systems and facilitate other software expansion.

The keyboard contains 32K RAM, expandable to 64K, and 24K ROM. The RAM adds capacity, allowing you to create and use larger programs; the ROM contains the Zgrass language and a scientific mathematics package. Either your television speaker or stereo sound system can be used to play back audio signals on the cassette, providing complete voice and music capability.

The keyboard has two standard RS-232 interfaces, two audio cassette interfaces, and a connector for a standard floppy disc. Available accessories include a printer; light pen (to draw directly on the screen); bit pad digitizer (to input artwork, maps, and models); floppy-disc drive; dual cassettes; slide

142

copier (that works with any single-lens reflex camera to create slides from the images on your TV screen); and sound system connection (to program music or sound effects under computer control to be played through your sound/stereo system).

ATARI COMPUTERS

Atari offers two personal/home computers: the Atari 400, an entry-level machine with a touch-sensitive keyboard designed for the home; and the Atari 800, a more sophisticated personal computer with a standard typewriter keyboard.

Atari 400

The Atari 400 (Fig. 6-18) is built around the 6502B micro-processor. The unit comes with 8K of RAM that can be expanded to a maximum of 16K. The 10K ROM operating system may be expanded to 26K with user-installed solid-state cartridge programs.

The 400 has a flat, touch-sensitive keyboard, plug connectors for external peripherals, and a built-in rf modulator that lets you attach the

Fig. 6-18. Atari 400 home computer. (Courtesy, Atari Co.)

If it looks like this push the switch to the **300 OHM (300Ω)** position

If it looks like this, loosen the screws holding the U-shaped slider and move it to the position marked **300 OHM or 300Ω**

If it looks like this screw the short round wire into the connector provided

To external
300 OHM Antenna

Fig. 6-19. Connecting the Atari 400 computer to the TV set.

computer to your own black-and-white or color television set. The unit features graphics in 16 colors, and there are four independent sound synthesizers for musical tones or game sounds that emanate from an internal speaker and the audio channels of your television set. You can connect game controls to the unit and add such peripherals as cassette recorder for program storage, a 40- or 80-column dot-matrix-impact printer, acoustic modem, and interface module.

The Atari 400 has excellent color graphics capability, with a maximum resolution of over 15,000 pixels; each of 16 colors can be displayed in any of eight intensity levels. A wide variety of programs is available to show off this capability, and you can program these with the built-in BASIC language interpreter. A TV switch box, a BASIC language cartridge, and various well-organized and clear instruction books/manuals are delivered with the Atari 400.

The software consists of an integral series of coded instructions. The foundation programs are supplied in the operating system ROM module; these activate the keyboard and the screen display, so you can create pictures and text, one "screenful" at a time. They also control the flow of all information within the computer, making it possible to add additional software through the keyboard, cartridges, or cassette tapes.

The second level of software is added to the computer by inserting a cartridge into the cartridge slot. The optional program recorder (a cassette recorder) provides an additional method of loading programs into the computer. The instructions for connecting the computer are simple. (Fig. 6-19.)

The keyboard generates 24 lines of 40 characters in upper- or lowercase; you can create inverse video and full-screen editing. The keyboard has alphanumeric, graphic, and control functions. Each key has the capacity to be redefined by instructions from an individual cartridge; this provides you with an efficient set of symbols for each computer application. (Fig. 6-20.)

Twenty-nine keys are used to create color graphics in 16 colors with a graphic resolution of 160 × 96 (320 × 192, requiring 16K RAM). Figure 6-21 illustrates which keys create a certain graphic symbol on the screen. Ten keys are used for screen editing (Fig. 6-22): that means that you can move the cursor anywhere on the screen and modify the display. These modifications let you erase all characters, insert a line or character, and delete a line or character. Finally, three keys are used to create special graphic characters (Fig. 6-23).

Peripherals and accessories that can be attached to the Atari 400 includes one or more joystick controllers, cassette recorder, printer, and interface module. Joysticks connect to the lower front of the computer console; each has one button and eight possible stick positions. Instructions in each cartridge program tell you how to operate each controller—which positions to use, and how to interpret the different elements of the display.

The program (cassette) recorder connects to the computer as shown in Fig. 6-24. Connections to the Atari 400 and 800 are similar.

To operate the recorder:

PLAY enables the computer to read the cassette. The tape will not move until the computer starts reading from the tape.

RECORD enables the computer to save programs or data on the cassette. You have to hold RECORD and PLAY together to enable the record mode.

STOP disengages the play or record modes.

EJECT opens the cassette door to release the cassette.

ADVANCE fast-winds the cassette forward.

REWIND fast-winds the cassette backward.

Fig. 6-20. Atari 400 keyboard layout. (Courtesy, Atari Co.)

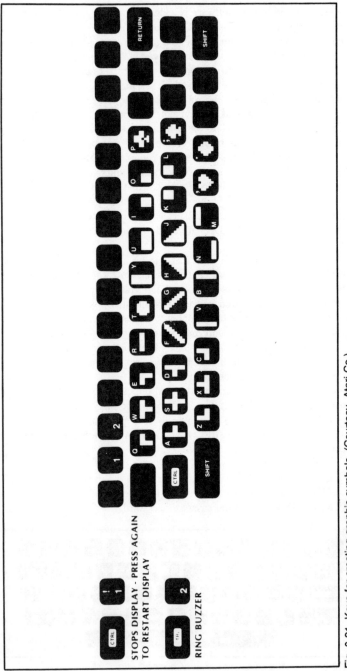

Fig. 6-21. Keys for creating graphic symbols. (Courtesy, Atari Co.)

146

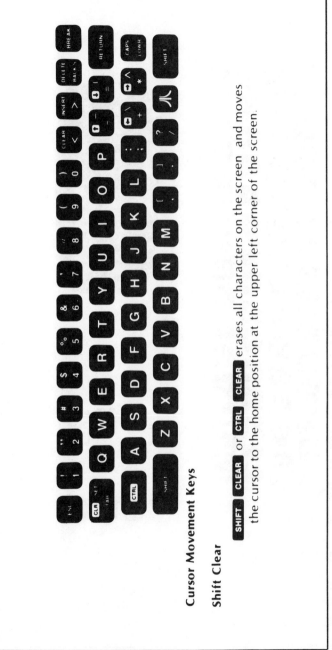

Cursor Movement Keys

Shift Clear

SHIFT CLEAR or CTRL CLEAR erases all characters on the screen and moves the cursor to the home position at the upper left corner of the screen.

Fig. 6-22. Ten editing keys used for editing purposes. (Courtesy, Atari Co.)

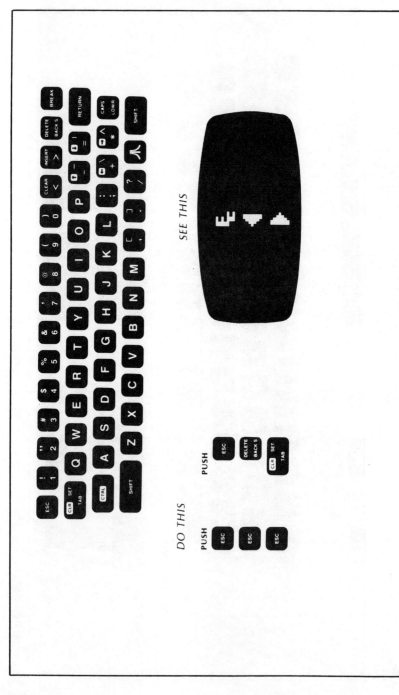

SEE THIS

DO THIS

PUSH

ESC · ESC · ESC

PUSH

ESC

DELETE BACK S

CLR SET TAB

148

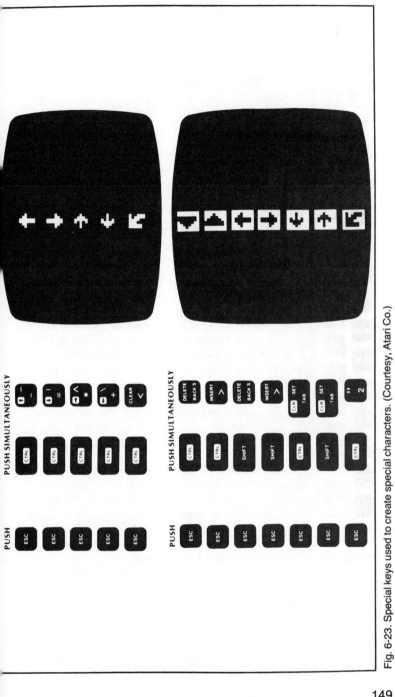

Fig. 6-23. Special keys used to create special characters. (Courtesy, Atari Co.)

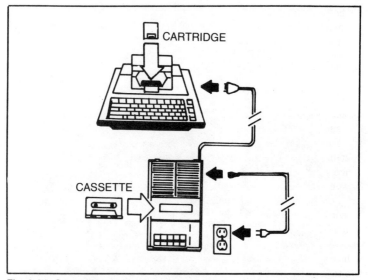

CARTRIDGE

CASSETTE

Fig. 6-24. Connecting the program recorder to the computer. (Courtesy, Atari Co.)

Some machines have a PAUSE key. This key leaves the machine in the play mode or record mode, but disengages the pinch roller from the tape.

The counter reset button sets the tape position counter to zero.

The Atari 850 Interface Module allows communication between the computer and RS-232C peripherals. This module connects between the computer console and the peripherals. (See Fig. 6-35.) The unit has four serial ports and one parallel port (which is referred to as the "printer port"). The interface module contains a microprocessor, memory, and programmable ports. The programming of the module is controlled from the computer system.

The manual for the module is very explicit, and emphasizes that communications between the peripheral and the computer must conform to the limitations imposed by the hardware. For example, the speed of communication is always limited. The limitations differ for different peripherals; the computer has to know what peripheral it's communicating with and how to compose and interpret messages to and from that peripheral. Some of that information is in computer memory, but initially it comes from a variety of sources. For example, the disc and disc drive are the sources of information for handling communications with the disc drive. The information is passed to the computer memory when the computer console is powered ON (provided the disc drive is itself already powered ON and contains a disc).

Information about the serial ports of the interface module is contained in the interface module itself and is transferred to computer memory when the computer is powered ON. Therefore, you must power the interface module

ON before you power the computer ON, if you intend to use a serial port. You may unnecessarily "boot the module"—that is, turn ON the module and then the computer, but then not use a serial port. This does no harm but it wastes RAM by loading the unused RS-232 handler.

The configuration and use of serial ports is a complex matter. In this area, you must keep a large number of details in mind and you must observe complicated procedures exactly. In its manual, Atari has tried to reduce the amount of technical detail, giving only what's necessary to show the structure and effect of commands and how they relate to each other.

You can use the interface module with non-Atari peripherals, but you must make sure that the device is compatible with the interface module. This device follows the standard that specifies electrical signal characteristics between a computer and its RS-232-compatible peripherals. (See Fig. 6-26.)

Looking at Fig. 6-26, you can see that a data terminal is at each end of the communication link. The data terminal either generates or receives data (or does both). It could be a keyboard/screen terminal in the normal sense of the word; it could be a computer, a.s.o. The idea is that the data terminal is at the end of the communication link—hence "terminal." However, since the data terminal doesn't really have to be at the end, you may find it easier to think of the data terminal as no more than a name for one of the two ends of an RS-232C connection.

At the other end of the RS-232C connection is the *data set*. Each such data set takes data from the data terminal it's connected to and sends/receives the data over the communication link. The most familiar example of a data set is the modem.

The distinction between data set and data terminal should be kept in mind because the RS-232C interface is *directional*—that is, each line in an RS-232C interface has a definite direction: one device drives the line (sends

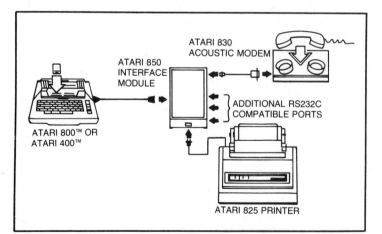

Fig. 6-25. Connecting the interface module to the computer system. (Courtesy, Atari Co.)

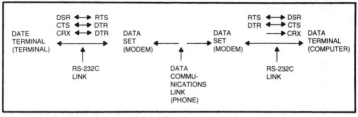

Fig. 6-26. Atari interface module. (Courtesy, Atari Co.)

information) and the other receives the information. Each line in an RS-232C interface is defined as being driven by either the data set end or the data terminal end.

A printer and acoustic modem can be attached to the Atari 850 Interface. The Atari 825 80-column printer is a dot-matrix impact printer that can print lines up to 8 inches long in three different character sets: normal, standard, and elongated. The printer operates under complete control of the Atari 400 or 800 computer. (The computer must of course be programmed to tell the printer what to do.)

The character sets (Fig. 6-27) are categorized as *monospaced* (10 cpi) (uniformly spaced) characters, at 10 characters per inch; *monospaced condensed* (condensed) characters, at 16.7 characters per inch; and *proportionally spaced* (proportional) characters, at an average 14 characters per inch. Each of these character sets consists of 96 standard ASCII characters. The printer is set to print monospaced characters when it's powered on; the condensed and proportionally spaced character sets must be programmed by the computer by means of control codes. (Incidentally, condensed and proportionally spaced characters can be mixed on the same line.)

The monospaced—10 cpi—and 16.7 cpi characters are formed in a dot matrix 7 dots wide by 8 dots high. The spacing between the characters is uniform: three spaces between 10 cpi monospaced characters and two spaces between the 16.7 cpi characters. Including the dot spaces between characters, the 10 cpi characters are considered to be 10 dot spaces, wide and the condensed characters 9 dot spaces wide.

The proportionally spaced characters are formed in a dot matrix n dots wide by 9 dots high, where n is a variable number of dots between 6 and 18.

Atari 800

This computer has a typewriter-style keyboard, built-in rf modulator, high-resolution graphics, and an internal speaker. The machine comes with 8K each of RAM and internal ROM, and a place for memory-expansion modules that can bring the computer up to a total of 48K RAM. External ROM can be expanded by 16K with cartridge programs. The software program is Atari BASIC.

In addition to the peripherals of the Atari 400 (cassette recorder, printer, modem, and interface module), the Atari 800 can have one

152

PROPORTIONAL NORMAL

!"#$%&'()*+,-./0123456789:;<=>?
@ABCDEFGHIJKLMNOPQRSTUVWXYZ[\]^_
`abcdefghijklmnopqrstuvwxyz{|}~

PROPORTIONAL ELONGAT

!"#$%&'()*+,-./0123456789:
@ABCDEFGHIJKLMNOPQRS
`abcdefghijklmnopqrstuvwxy

10 CPI NORMAL

!"#$%&'()*+,-./0123456789:;<=>?
@ABCDEFGHIJKLMNOPQRSTUVWXYZ[\]^_
`abcdefghijklmnopqrstuvwxyz{|}^

10 CFI ELONGATED

!"#$%&'()*+,-./012
@ABCDEFGHIJKLMNOPQR
`abcdefghijklmnopqr

CONDENSED (16.7 CPI) NORMAL

!"#$%&'()*+,-./0123456789:;<=>?
@ABCDEFGHIJKLMNOPQRSTUVWXYZ[\]^_
`abcdefghijklmnopqrstuvwxyz{|}^

CONDENSED (16.7 CPI) ELONGATED

!"#$%&'()*+,-./0123456789:;<=>?
@ABCDEFGHIJKLMNOPQRSTUVWXYZ[\]^_
`abcdefghijklmnopqrstuvwxyz{|}^

Fig. 6-27. Character sets of Atari 825 printer. (Courtesy, Atari Co.)

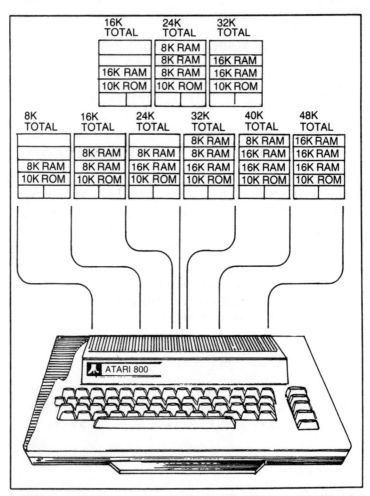

Fig. 6-28. Expanding the memory capacity of the Atari 800 by means of inserting modules. (Courtesy, Atari Co.)

to four minidisc drives storing from 96 to 368K bytes of on-line data storage. The keyboard layout of the 800 is similar to that of the 400, including all the various functions assigned to the keys. The cassette recorder, too, is connected in the same way it's connected to the Atari 400.

With the basic system of 8K RAM memory and the program recorder, the 800 system configuration can accommodate all the preprogrammed cartridges and cassettes that make up the Atari 8K library. Any program in the 8K library may be used with the Atari 400, 800, and expanded 800 computers.

The expansion of the Atari 800 can be accomplished with one or more

8K or 16K memory modules. With the operating system 10K ROM in socket 0, you can add various combination modules in the remaining sockets 1, 2, and 3 (Fig. 6-28). With an expanded 16K capacity, you can use the larger, more sophisticated programs from the 16K library.

The Atari 800 lets you connect up to four floppy-disc drives. (Figure 6-29 illustrates the connection to one such disc drive.) When you look at the rear of the disc drive, you'll note two I/O connectors. One is used to connect the first drive to the computer, and the other to connect (or *daisy-chain*) number one drive to number two, and so on, up to a total of four drives.

The Atari disc-drive manual is very well organized: for example, instructions on how to handle the discs are unusually explicit. (See Fig. 6-30.) The disc drives offer you the capability to store and retrieve programs; create and add to data files needed by programs; make copies of disc files; erase old files from a disc; load and save binary files; and move files to and from memory, the screen, disc, printer, or any other new peripheral Atari may introduce.

Since the actual operation of a floppy disc has been discussed at some length earlier in the book, we won't elaborate on this further.

Figure 6-31 illustrates the Atari 800, and Fig. 6-32 shows it interfacing with its various peripherals. Just how easy the installations are with the Atari 800 computer is illustrated in Fig. 6-33 (Atari 800 with cassette recorder and disc drive) and Fig. 6-34 (computer with disc drive, printer, and cassette recorder).

CASIO

This year Casio will introduce the FX-9000P—an 8080A-based computer with a packaging that closely resembles that of the Hewlett-Packard

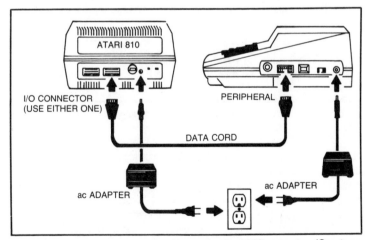

Fig. 6-29. Connecting a floppy-disc drive to the Atari 800 computer. (Courtesy, Atari Co.)

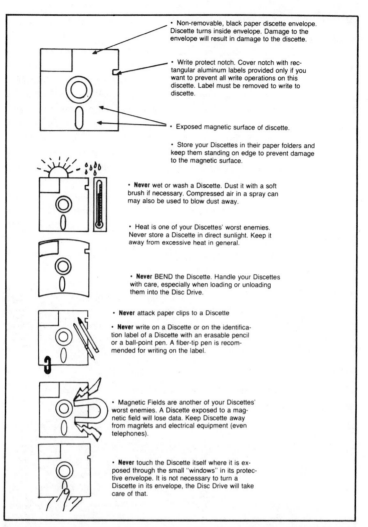

- Non-removable, black paper discette envelope. Discette turns inside envelope. Damage to the envelope will result in damage to the discette.

- Write protect notch. Cover notch with rectangular aluminum labels provided only if you want to prevent all write operations on this discette. Label must be removed to write to discette.

- Exposed magnetic surface of discette.

- Store your Discettes in their paper folders and keep them standing on edge to prevent damage to the magnetic surface.

- **Never** wet or wash a Discette. Dust it with a soft brush if necessary. Compressed air in a spray can may also be used to blow dust away.

- Heat is one of your Discettes' worst enemies. Never store a Discette in direct sunlight. Keep it away from excessive heat in general.

- **Never** BEND the Discette. Handle your Discettes with care, especially when loading or unloading them into the Disc Drive.

- **Never** attack paper clips to a Discette

- **Never** write on a Discette or on the identification label of a Discette with an erasable pencil or a ball-point pen. A fiber-tip pen is recommended for writing on the label.

- Magnetic Fields are another of your Discettes' worst enemies. A Discette exposed to a magnetic field will lose data. Keep Discette away from magnets and electrical equipment (even telephones).

- **Never** touch the Discette itself where it is exposed through the small "windows" in its protective envelope. It is not necessary to turn a Discette in its envelope, the Disc Drive will take care of that.

Fig. 6-30. Atari manual's instructions how to handle floppy discs. (Courtesy, Atari Co.)

HP-85 we'll discuss later on in this book. A built-in high-resolution 5-in. CRT display with 32 characters by 16 lines (256 × 128 pixels) is capable of mixed text and graphic applications. The unit has ROM BASIC, and the built-in 8K RAM can be expanded with plug-in modules. You can choose between 16K dynamic RAM cartridges or 4K RAM cartridges with battery backup.

A tape cassette interface is available, and a real-time clock and calendar/alarm. Several parallel and serial interfaces allow you to connect printers, disc drives, and modems.

COMMODORE INTERNATIONAL LTD.

Commodore Business Machines offers a number of personal computers, but for our purposes we'll concentrate on the PET personal/home computer and the VIC-20 personal/home computer. The **PET**—short for Personal Electronic Translator—2001 is a very attractive machine built around the 6502 microprocessor. It has 8K of standard RAM, with an expansion up to 32K RAM. Operating system ROM is 14K, with an expansion to 22K.

The keyboard has alphanumeric keypads, providing four connections, two cassette recorders, a parallel I/O device, and an IEEE-488-compatible I/O device. A high-resolution 9-in. screen provides graphics and text in an easy-to-read green coloration.

The **VIC-20** is Commodore's latest entry in the low-priced computer market. Priced at under $300, the VIC (Video Interface Computer) connects to your TV or monitor. It comes with 5K of RAM (expandable to 32K) and 27K of ROM. In addition to its color capability and full-sized typewriter keyboard with programmable function keys, the VIC-20 features a sound device, external expansion ports, and a 506-character screen display - 22

Fig. 6-31. Atari 800 computer. (Courtesy, Atari Co.)

157

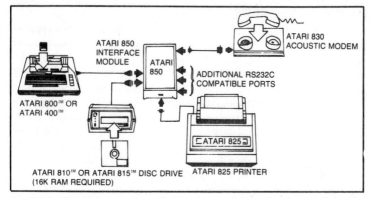

Fig. 6-32. Atari 800 computer with interface module and various peripherals. (Courtesy, Atari Co.)

characters by 23 lines. The machine is equipped with standard PET BASIC and a graphics character set for generating high-resolution graphics - 176 × 176, or 30,976 pixels.

There are three ways to store data on the VIC-20: tape, disc, and cartridge. A tape cassette interface allows you to connect the computer to a cassette recorder. A single floppy-disc unit provides up to 170K of additional memory storage.

Two kinds of cartridges are available for data storage: auto-starting cartridges that activate as soon as they are plugged in, and cartridges that must be turned ON by means of an access command. The cartridges are contained in 3K, 8K, and 16K memory expanders, and a 4-slot multiplexer accepts these memory cartridges, program cartridges, and/or IEEE devices. A superexpander provides high-resolution graphics, music, and 3K of memory. Among peripherals that can be connected are a dot-matrix printer; such game controls as joysticks, paddles, and light pen; and an RS-232C modem interface.

Let's take a look at the keyboard of this really amazing, inexpensive computer (Fig. 6-35) and note the following:

Graphics and the COMMODORE Key. When you turn the computer on you're automatically in graphics mode, which means you can type uppercase characters and the more than 60 graphic keys. There are two graphics on each key. To get the graphic on the right side, simply hold down the SHIFT key and type the key with the graphic you want. To get the graphics on the left side, hold down the COMMODORE key (the little flag) and you can type uppercase letters and the full graphics at the same time.

Upper and Lowercase and Graphics. To get into the text mode, you simply press the SHIFT and COMMODORE keys together. This allows you to use the machine as an ordinary typewriter, with full upper- and lowercase letters, plus all the graphics on the left side of the keys—the graphics most suited for preparing charts and graphs.

Color. You can change the colors of the characters you type by pressing the CTRL key and any one of the eight color/number keys. The colors are black, white, red, cyan, purple, green, blue, and yellow. (You can set and change colors inside or outside a computer program.) In addition to the eight character colors, you can also change the colors of the border and screen on your television set by typing a special command called a "POKE." For example, if you type the command POKE 36879,X (with X some number from 1 to 255), you can get up to 255 different combinations of screen and border colors, including 16 screen colors and eight border colors.

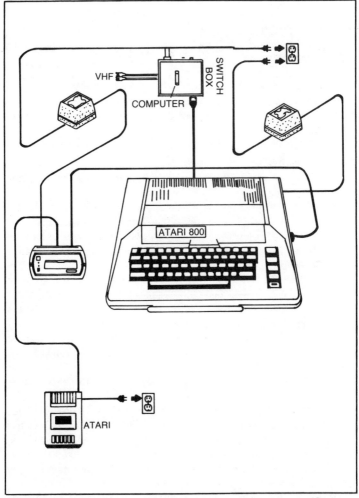

Fig. 6-33. Atari 800 computer with disc drive and cassette recorder. (Courtesy, Atari Co.)

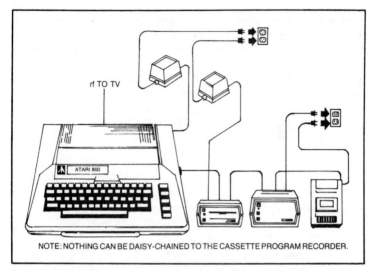

NOTE: NOTHING CAN BE DAISY-CHAINED TO THE CASSETTE PROGRAM RECORDER.

Fig. 6-34. Atari 800 computer with disc drive, printer, and cassette recorder. (Courtesy, Atari Co.)

Special Editing Keys

Following are some of the other special keys that make this computer such a full-featured one.

CTRL. Used to set character colors, and—in conjunction with such special programs as word processing—to execute special commands.

Run/Stop. This key lets you automatically load programs into the computer's memory from a cassette tape. Hitting this key without shifting interrupts a running program.

Shift. The VIC-20 has two SHIFT keys and a SHIFT LOCK key, just like a typewriter, for typing long strings of uppercase letters or graphics.

RVS ON/RVS OFF. These two keys let you type reverse characters on the screen (inverse video).

CLR/HOME. This key moves the cursor to the home position at the top left-hand corner of the screen. If you type SHIFT and CLR/HOME, you clear the screen of all the characters.

INST/DEL. This editing key allows you to insert or delete characters—as when you've made a mistake, for example.

RESTORE. This is a "reset" key. If you press the RUN/STOP and RESTORE keys together, you completely reset the computer, as if you had just turned it on. Programs you had in memory are retained, however, and can be listed or run from the start.

Cursor Keys. These give you the ability to move the cursor into any position on the screen—up or down, left or right.

Return. This key is used primarily for entering commands and instructions to the computer.

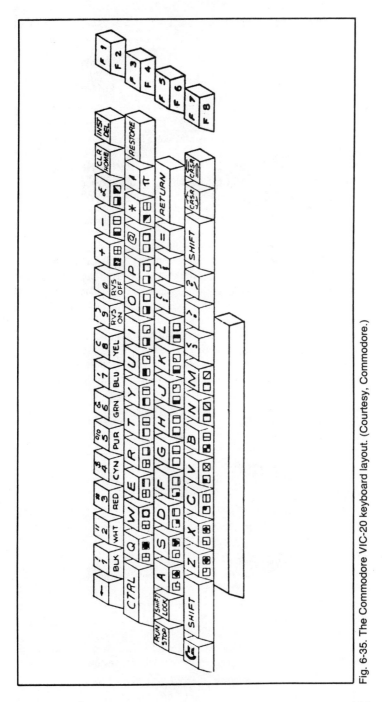

Fig. 6-35. The Commodore VIC-20 keyboard layout. (Courtesy, Commodore.)

Programmable Function Keys. These four keys with shift capability on the far right side of the keyboard allow you eight functions. You may assign any BASIC command or instruction to these keys under program control.

Looking at the keyboard, it should be clear that the unit allows for gradual simple expansion without the need for a lot of accessories. (See Fig. 6-36.) The USER PORT and CASSETTE PORT allow for connection to a modem and cassette drive. The SERIAL BUS permits a floppy-disc drive and printer to connect in daisy-chain fashion. The VIDEO OUTPUT connects to your television set or monitor. The EXPANSION PORT provides you with the opportunity to expand the memory of the computer, while the GAME PORT allows the use of joystick, light pen, or paddles.

The bottom line: this is a good machine for the price.

EXIDY CORPORATION

The Exidy Sorcerer Computer is housed in a typewriter-style keyboard, built around the Z80 microprocessor. Memory is either 16, 32, or 48K bytes of RAM and 16K bytes of ROM. The video output provides 1920 characters in a 30-line-by-64-character display, and graphics of 512 × 240 pixels. The keyboard is alphanumeric with special function keys. Additional I/O accommodates a serial port (modem), parallel port (for a printer), dual cassette, and expansion interface. (See Fig. 6-37).

Peripherals include the following:

Video Display Unit. This is mounted on a swivel base (see Fig. 6-38).

Display Disc. Same as video display above, except that two floppy-disc drives are built in, providing a total of 1.2 megabytes of additional storage. (See Fig. 6-39.)

S-100 Interface. This device allows you to connect up to six expansion interfaces, such as speed synthesizers, music producers, Winchester hard-disc drives, and others. (See Fig. 6-40.)

Disc Drives. Available drives include a 5¼-inch single-sided floppy-disc drive that connects directly to the computer system; an 8-in. floppy-disc drive; and a 10-megabyte Winchester disc drive.

Printers. Possibilities include daisy-wheel, dot-matrix, and graphics printer.

HEWLETT-PACKARD

The HP-85 is built around a custom-designed proprietary NMOS microprocessor and a powerful BASIC language that integrate the various elements into a unitary computer system. The system, which is the size of a portable typewriter, contains the microprocessor, typewriter-like keyboard, five-inch video monitor, thermal printer, and tape cartridge. The unit also has graphics functions. The system has four I/O ports that hold a range of optional interfaces that let you expand the system with printers, disc drives, and other peripherals. (See Fig. 6-41.)

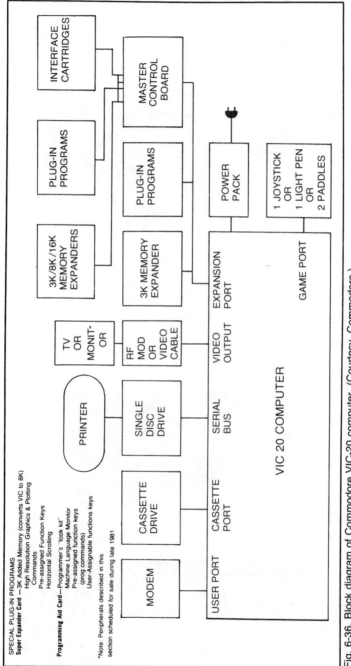

SPECIAL PLUG-IN PROGRAMS
Super Expander Card —3K Added Memory (converts VIC to 8K)
High Resolution Graphics & Plotting
Commands
Pre-assigned Function Keys
Horizontal Scrolling
Programming Aid Card—Programmer's "took kit"
Machine Language Monitor
Pre-assigned function keys
(prog commands)
User-Assignable functions keys

*Note: Peripherals described in this
section scheduled for sale during late 1981

INTERFACE CARTRIDGES

PLUG-IN PROGRAMS

PLUG-IN PROGRAMS

3K/8K/16K MEMORY EXPANDERS

MASTER CONTROL BOARD

POWER PACK

1 JOYSTICK OR 1 LIGHT PEN OR 2 PADDLES

3K MEMORY EXPANDER

EXPANSION PORT

GAME PORT

TV OR MONIT-OR

RF MOD OR VIDEO CABLE

VIDEO OUTPUT

PRINTER

SINGLE DISC DRIVE

SERIAL BUS

CASSETTE DRIVE

CASSETTE PORT

MODEM

USER PORT

VIC 20 COMPUTER

Fig. 6-36. Block diagram of Commodore VIC-20 computer. (Courtesy, Commodore.)

163

Fig. 6-37. Exidy Sorcerer computer system. (Courtesy, Exidy Corporation.)

The system has 16K of RAM, which can be expanded to 32K by plugging an optional memory module into one of the ports. Resident are 32K bytes of ROM, expandable with up to six 8K-byte ROM modules. The keyboard has a total of 92 keys, each designed to perform a certain function.

Fig. 6-38. Exidy Sorcerer computer with video display. (Courtesy, Exidy Corporation).

Fig. 6-39. Exidy Sorcerer computer with video display/floppy-disc drive combination. (Courtesy, Exidy Corporation.)

This keyboard is divided into four sets of functions: *typewriter board*, for entering letters and the like; *numeric keypad*, for entering numbers and doing arithmetic operations; *control keys* that are assigned functions by you during program development; and *display, editing, and system-control keys* to control the CRT, operating system, tape drive, and printer.

The screen displays 16 lines by 32 characters, and in the graphics mode displays 256 × 192 dot field. The thermal printer prints upper- and lowercase characters at 32 character lines per second.

Fig. 6-40. S-100 Interface unit for Sorcerer computer. (Courtesy, Exidy Corporation.)

Fig. 6-41. The HP-85 personal computer. (Courtesy, Hewlett-Packard.)

The built-in tape drive uses HP data cartridges, each with a capacity of 217K bytes. The computer automatically sets up a tape directory at the beginning of each tape, allowing you to find exact locations of recorded programs and data.

Add-on mass storage is enormous, if not phenomenal. Using four floppy-disc drives—5¼, double-sided, double-density—you can add 1,080K bytes master unit, a single (one-drive) master unit, a dual add-on, and a single add-on. Using 4 8-inch, double-density floppy-disc drives, you can add up to 4,720K bytes of memory storage. The drives include a dual master, a single master, a dual add-on, and a single add-on.

Other peripherals include:

● **Dot-matrix impact printer** (7 × 9 dot-matrix; 132 characters per line on 8½"-wide paper; 180 characters per second).

● **Graphics plotter** (Connected to the computer, lets you produce publication-quality plots to sharpen analysis of presentations and reports; see unit on the right of Fig. 6-42 and Fig. 6-43).

● **Graphics tablet** (Lets you interact with the graphics display of the computer. As you move the pen-like stylus around the tablet (see Fig. 6-42, *left*), the tablet translates your movements into digital code and transmits this code to the computer. Points are entered continuously as you draw, or whenever the stylus is pressed down.)

● **Software** is business/scientific-oriented.

IBM

At first glance, the IBM Personal Computer system (Fig. 6-44) may look like a revolutionary product. Taken feature by feature, however, the

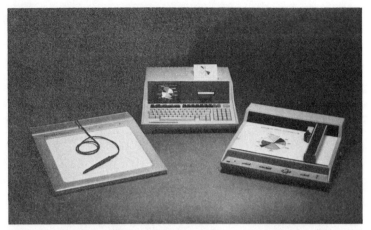

Fig. 6-42. HP-85 personal computer (*center*) with graphics tablet (*left*) and plotter (*right*). (Courtesy, Hewlett-Packard.)

IBM offers little that can't be found in other personal computers. The real distinction of this system is the way these features have been incorporated into one product.

The IBM Personal Computer has four major elements: the system unit, which contains the processor and one or two 5¼ inch discette drives; a

Fig. 6-43. HP-85 personal computer with plotter in use to create hard-copy graphics. (Courtesy, Hewlett-Packard.)

Fig. 6-44. IBM Personal Computer. (Courtesy, IBM Corporation.)

detached 83-key keyboard; a high-resolution monochrome display; and a wire matrix printer. In addition, a variety of options are offered. There are two display adapters—one for the monochrome display, the other for color and graphics displays. A discette card allows up to four double-density discette drives to be connected to the system. Storage cards of 32 KB or 64 KB may be added to increase memory size to 256 KB. An asynchronous communications card can attach a variety of devices using the RS232-C standard. The printer adapter card provides a parallel port for the attachment of a printer; the game control adapter will connect joysticks or paddles to the system. These cards may be installed in any of the five system expansion slots on the system board.

Software

On the software side, the system unit has 40 KB of ROM containing a powerful BASIC interpreter, and the Basic I/O System (BIOS) to control the standard and optional system devices. In addition, the disc-operating system (DOS) opens the door to a variety of programs, including advanced versions of the BASIC interpreter. Many applications are already available.

Game Control Adapter

The game control adapter allows the system to attach paddles or joysticks—up to four paddles or two joysticks, a total of four resistive inputs. Four switch inputs are also available on the card. The paddle position is determined by timing an RC network containing the paddle resistor. This digital value is proportional to the paddle position.

The BASIC interpreter contained within the system ROM allows direct interrogation of all four paddle positions. The Advanced BASIC allows the switch inputs to cause ON conditions to be executed within the BASIC program, allowing immediate reaction to switch input. This is one reason why games for the IBM Personal Computer are family favorites (Fig. 6-45).

INTERTEC DATA SYSTEMS

The SuperBrain Video Computer System, first introduced by Intertec in 1979, features twin Z80A microprocessors. One processor—known as the host—performs all processor- and screen-related functions, while the second processor is used mainly to execute disc I/O. (When not processing disc data, this second microprocessor may be programmed for other related functions.) Although the SuperBrain is basically a single-board computer—it does not have the traditional motherboard, with plug-in slots

Fig. 6-45. The IBM Personal Computer is a favorite of all family members. (Courtesy, IBM Corporation.)

Fig. 6-46. Mattel Intellivision home computer system. (Courtesy, Mattel Electronics.)

for CPU, RAM, etc.—it does have sufficient space inside for a single S-100-compatible board. This is often occupied by the disc controller, but you can add anything you like from among available accessories.

The display screen is built into the unit, providing 25 80-character lines on a 12-in. screen. The keyboard is alphanumeric with 128 upper- and lowercase ASCII characters. The Cp/M operating system has 2K ROM memory, and there is 32K RAM expandable to 64K [the model QD has 64K RAM] in 32K increments.

Also built into the system are two double-density, single-sided floppy-disc drives with 350K of memory storage, text editor, assembler, program debugger, and disc formatter. Two RS-232C ports for serial data transmission via a modem or a serial printer are standard with the unit. Finally, CompuStar 10-megabyte disc-storage system (DSS), featuring an 8-in. Winchester drive, can be attached to the SuperBrain.

MATTEL ELECTRONICS INC.

The Mattel's Intellivision is a computer keyboard, called Keyboard Component, that attaches to the existing Master Component Video Game Machine. The machine will soon be available with the following specifications:

●The keyboard is a 60-key typewriter-style board that,combined with the Master Component, offers 16K RAM with an expansion to 8 megabytes. The keyboard has a built-in cassette recorder, and when connected to a television set or monitor provides 24 lines of 40 characters of text and 160 by 192 pixels with 16 colors. The Master Component has two hand controllers, a 12-button numeric keypad, four action keys, and a 16-direction object-movement disc.

●Two parallel peripheral I/O ports allow for expansion with such peripherals as a 40-column printer, modem, and voice synthesizer. In the area of software, the following programs have been developed: income-tax preparation, stock analysis, physical conditioning, music composition, astrology, speed reading, weight-loss program, and conversational French.

Figure 6-46 illustrates the combined components.

NIPPON ELECTRIC COMPANY

The PC-8001 personal computer from NEC is a stand-alone system consisting of a keyboard built around the Z-80 microprocessor (the NEC equivalent of PD780). (See Fig. 6-42.)

The 82-key alphanumeric keyboard provides upper- and lowercase characters—20 to 25 lines by 80 characters. The rear panel of the keyboard allows you to make any of five connections: to the NEC monitor model JB-1201M; to an rf modulator, for connection to your television set; to a cassette interface; to a Centronics-type printer/parallel interface; or to a serial interface for modem use.

The unit is supplied with a standard 24K ROM and 16K RAM—both expandable to 32K. The operating system is N-BASIC. When connected to the NEC monitor (Fig. 6-48), the computer provides a 248-symbol character set. The graphic function is 16 × 100 matrix, with eight colors; black, blue, red, magenta, green, cyan, yellow, white.

The NEC PC-8012A interface unit has seven slots for expansion boards. The unit allows you to expand memory to 128K RAM and additional ROM capacity. You can also use it to connect to two RS-232C-compatible

Fig. 6-47. Keyboard of PC-8001. (Courtesy, NEC America.)

171

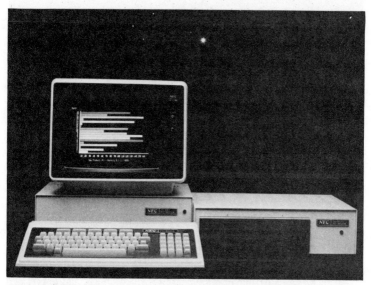

Fig. 6-48. PC-8001 computer connected to monitor and interface unit. (Courtesy, NEC America.)

peripherals, or attach a floppy-disc drive. Finally, you can use its unit to connect to four parallel peripherals or to an IEEE-488-compatible accessory.

The NEC PC-8031A dual floppy-disc drives—single-sided, double-density—allow you additional external memory of 143K per unit, or 286 bytes total. A second pair of disc drives can be daisy-chained.

The computer has two modes of operation: BASIC and terminal. The BASIC mode allows you to use the machine as a stand-alone personal computer. In the terminal mode, the machine acts like a terminal that can be connected to a modem.

Color and graphics capability are excellent. The range of available software programs would seem to indicate that the unit is directed to the serious personal-computer user, rather than to the more casual home user.

OHIO SCIENTIFIC INC. (OSI)

Ohio Scientific presently provides one of the widest product lines in the industry, ranging from a small personal computer to a conventionally packaged minicomputer. There are basically two "Challenger Series"— Challenger I and Challenger 2. To avoid confusion, however, we'll only indicate model numbers in our descriptions.

C1P

This is a self-contained computer with full computer-style keyboard; video-display interface, with graphics; cassette interface; and BASIC in

Fig. 6-49. C1P self-contained computer. (Courtesy, Ohio Scientific Inc.)

ROM. There are 10K bytes in ROM; 8K bytes in RAM (expandable to 32K bytes). The keyboard has 53 keys with upper- and lowercase and user programmability. Graphics are 256 × 256 points. Characters are displayed in 24 lines by 24 characters, or 12 × 48, and up to 32 × 32 or 16 × 64 with specially modified closed-circuit monitors. (See Fig. 6-49).

Sound, music, and voice output is available via digital-to-analog converter. You can attach a cassette recorder, 300-baud modem, and printer to the computer via the appropriate interfaces. Finally, you can choose from 120 software cassettes in the areas of education, entertainment, personal use, and small businesses.

C1P MF

This unit has the same features as the C1P but includes some additional capabilities (Fig. 6-50). For example, a real-time clock provides timing and time of day information in conjunction with programs.

Memory storage is 10K bytes ROM and 20K bytes RAM, expandable to 32K bytes RAM. The addition of a floppy-disc drive expands data-storage capability by another 90K bytes. You can also attach a second disc drive, color display (the C1P has black-and-white only) joysticks, and ac remote control for lights and appliance and home security.

An I/O expander is used to provide the following additional capabilities to either the C1P or C1P MF:

- Composite color outputs with up to 16 colors.
- Dual 8-axis joystick interface.
- Dual remote 10-key pad interface.
- Ac remote-control interface.
- Home security interface.
- 16-line parallel I/O interface.
- Programmable sound generator.
- Program-selectable modem and high-speed printer interface port.

C4P DF

This is a fully integrated small computer system with a full 53-keyboard, color video display interface with elaborate graphics capability, high-speed operation, ample disc-storage capacity, and a large applications software library. (See Fig. 6-57.) Memory is 52K bytes total ROM/RAM standard with 48K RAM yielding 36K bytes program workspace under the operating system OS-65D, expandable to a total of 96K RAM.

Standard dual 8-in. floppy-disc drives store an additional 600K bytes of information. An optional double-sided disc drive expands the storage to 1.2 million bytes. The display provides 32 lines by 64 characters in upper- and lowercase. Graphic elements have an effective screen resolution of 256 by 512 points (pixels) with up to 16 colors.

Built-in I/O offers:

- RS-232C port for 300-baud modem.
- RS-232C port for 300/1200-baud printer.
- Two 8-axis joystick interfaces.
- Two 10-key pad interfaces.
- Ac remote control interface for lights and appliances.
- Home-security system interface.
- Eight-bit DAC for sound, music, and voice output.
- Programmable sound generator.
- Sixteen Parallel I/O lines.
- Sixteen-line I/O port for use with external 48-line I/O card, PROM blaster, 12-bit AD/DA module, and educational hardware development.

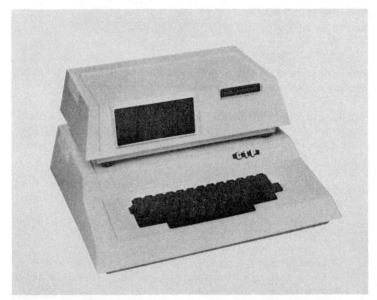

Fig. 6-50. C1P MF computer system. (Courtesy, Ohio Scientific Inc.)

Fig. 6-51. C4P DF computer system. (Courtesy, Ohio Scientific Inc.)

● Real-time clock standard.

Extensive entertainment, education, and personal software programs are available.

C4P MF

This computer has all the features of the previously described C4P DF, except that it has one single mini-floppy-disc drive and comes with only 24K bytes of RAM. (See Fig. 6-52.) Like the C4P DF, it's a cassette recorder-based system, and offering more than 120 cassette titles for education, entertainment, personal use, and small business.
The I/O capabilities for this computer include:

● Two 8-axis joystick interfaces.
● Two 8-key pad interfaces.
● Sound generator.
● DAC for sound, music, and voice output.
● Ac remote-control interface to control lights and appliances.
● Audio cassette, modem, printer interface.

C8P

This machine is similar to the C4P, but is housed in a larger case to allow for greater expansion.

C8P DF

This is the computer system graciously lent to me by Ohio Scientific so that I could familiarize myself with the actual workings of a computer. Consequently, we'll be examining it at some length and in some detail.

This system—consists of a number of modules, as follows:

- 53-key keyboard
- Color monitor
- Dual floppy-disc system (8-in. single-sided discs)
- Two joysticks
- Dot-matrix printer
- Telephone data coupler
- Complete home alarm and security system (described later)

See Fig. 6-52.

Installation was simple, following the easy illustrations and step-by-step instructions (Fig. 6-54). This particular system didn't have an A15 cable, so I had to open the cover of both the computer and disc-drive system in order to make the proper connections; however, since everything was properly labeled, no problems were encountered. The only tool needed was a flat-head screwdriver to remove the covers; all connections are prewired with connectors. Figure 6-55 illustrates the connection between computer and disc system.

With the system connected, the computer was turned on (via the switch on the rear panel) and reset with the reset button located on the front panel. The disc drive was turned on (again, by a switch on the rear panel), and reset similarly to the computer. The video monitor was turned on.

On the keyboard, two keys have to be actuated: the SHIFT LOCK key, which has to remain in its depressed position all the time; and the BREAK key. (See Fig. 6-56.) After insertion of the disc, the computer responded with "H/D/M," and after typing D, the program was viewed on the screen. It was a continuous execution of all the computer's capabilities, especially its color graphics. A continuously moving pattern developed that was fascinating to watch.

Next, the CUSTOMER DEMO DISC was viewed. With nine programs on the disc, the game TIGER TANK was tried. I lost twice, with the computer chiding me that using my "eyes a little better next time" would

Fig. 6-52. C4P MF computer system. (Courtesy, Ohio Scientific Inc.)

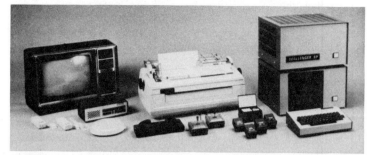

Fig. 6-53. The C8P DF computer system used by this writer. *Left foreground*: home security system. *Rear*: video display monitor. *Center front*: modem and joysticks. *Rear*: printer. *Right foreground*: home light control system and keyboard. *Reartop*: computer system. *Rear bottom*: double floppy-disc drive system. (Courtesy, Ohio Scientific Inc.)

increase my chances of winning. For brainless creatures, computers can sometimes manage to have the last word!

The first thing to do before operating any computer is to learn the keyboard, the various commands, and the list of errors. Although I'm talking about the C8P DF, that rule applies to any computer.

The keyboard consists of rows and columns of conductors; when a key is depressed, contact between the row conductor and the column conductor is made. To determine whether or not a key is depressed, certain values can be entered into the keyboard address by a POKE command and the results observed by a PEEK command. (POKE is a BASIC instruction used to place a value (poke) into any location in programmable memory; PEEK is a BASIC instruction that allows you to look (or peek) at any location in programmable memory. This latter instruction is often used to scan the memory locations that hold the information displayed on the video monitor, in order to determine what's being displayed.)

The keyboard is laid out like a regular typewriter QWERT, with some additional keys:

SHIFT LOCK. This key forces uppercase letters to be printed on the CRT. It should remain in depressed position when running BASIC programs.

BREAK. Resets the computer any time after the system is powered up.

SPACE [Bar]. Provides a space when pressed.

RETURN. Must be pressed after a line is typed, or in order for a final command to be initiated.

CONTROL + C. When pressed simultaneously, the program listing or execution is interrupted and the message BREAK IN LINE XXX is printed. (XXX is a line number in the program.)

SHIFT + O. When pressing SHIFT first while simultaneously pressing O, the last character typed will be erased.

177

SHIFT + P. Same as above, but the current line being typed will be erased.

D. When pressed after BREAK, it causes initialization of the computer and boots the operating from the disc drive.

M. Same as above, except the computer is initialized in its machine-language monitor.

Statements allow you to transfer data in and out of your program. A statement is actually a command (more precisely, an instruction) to the computer. Each statement is preceded by a *line number*, so that the computer can use the order of these numbers to determine the order in

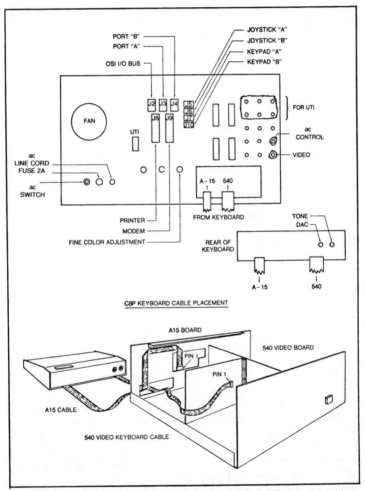

Fig. 6-54. Installation instructions and connections of C8P DF computer system. (Courtesy, Ohio Scientific Inc.)

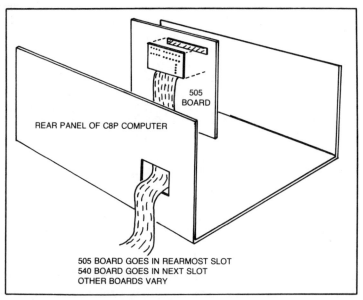

Fig. 6-55. Connecting cable between computer and disc drive.

which to execute the instructions in your statements. The OSI C8P DF statements are shown in Table 6-1.

Commands may be typed in without being preceded by a line number. When a command is entered, the computer performs the required tasks immediately. Many statements may also be entered as commands:

LIST	Lists the program.
NULL	Eliminates carriage rebounce return.
RUN	Starts program execution at first line.
NEW	Deletes current program.
CONT	Continues program after CONTROL + C or STOP if the program has not been modified.
LOAD	Used in DISC BASIC only.

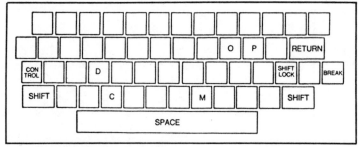

Fig. 6-56. C8P DF keyboard layout.

179

Table 6-1. OSI C8P DF Statements

Name	Example	Comments
INPUT	10 INPUT A	Variable A will be accepted from the terminal.
DEF	10 DEF FNA (V)=V*B	User-defined function of one argument.
DIM	110 (DIM A (12)	Allocates space for matrices and sets all matrix variables to zero. Nondimensioned variables default to 10.
END	999 END	Terminates program.
FOR, NEXT	10 FOR X= 1 to 10 STEP 1 20 30 NEXT X	STEP is needed only when X is not incremented by 1. NEXT X is needed only FOR NEXT loops are nested, if not, NEXT alone can be used.
GOTO	50 GOTO 100	Jumps to line 100.
GOSUB RETURN	100 GOSUB 500 500 . . . . . . 600 RETURN	Goes to subroutine, RETURN goes back to next line number after the GOSUB.
IF . . . THEN	10 IF X=5 THEN 5 10 IF X=5 THEN PRINT X 10 IF X=5 THEN PRINT X:Y=7	Standard IF-THEN conditional with the option to do multiple statements.

IF . . . GOTO	10 IF X=5 GOTO 5	Same as IF-THEN with line number.
ON . . . GOTO	100 on 1 GOTO 10,20	Computed GOTO. IF I=1 then 10 IF I=2 then 20
DATA	10 DATA 1,3,7	Data for READ statements must be in order to be read. Strings may be read in DATA statements.
PRINT	10 PRINT X 20 PRINT "Test"	Prints value of expression. Standard BASIC syntax with " " formats.
READ	490 READ V,W	Reads data consecutively from DATA statements in program.
REM	10 REM	This is an abbreviation of REMARKS, for nonexecuted commands.
RESTORE	500 RESTORE	Restores initial values of all data statements.
STOP	100 STOP	Stops program execution, reports a BREAK. Program can be restarted via CONT.

Armed with this knowledge, the canned program OS-65D was put through its paces. The menu-oriented system—an applications disc printing a directory of files present on the disc—provided operational messages; also, as a disc utility program it contained a menu of available BASIC programs. This OSI disc operating system is convenient for beginners to use in programming in BASIC: it supports writing programs in BASIC, storing programs on disc, recalling programs, and reading and writing sequential and random-access data files in BASIC. An extensive manual was extremely helpful with the fundamental operation of the system.

In writing your own programs, or adding to or deleting from existing ones, you learn fast to recognize the error codes that appear on the display, such as SN (syntax error, typo, etc.) and OV (overflow—the result of entering a calculation too large for BASIC).

The next program that was utilized was the Planner Plus, which is basically a financial modeling program. In financial modeling, profit can be measured as a function of monthly sales, and net income as a function of inflation. It's therefore a very useful program for the home budgeter.

The software, consisting of a number of floppy discs, allowed the following programming:

Line Editor. Used to enter and edit the model's item list.

Column Editor. Used to enter and edit the model's frame of reference.

Immediate Mode. Used to enter data, test assumptions, and execute the completed model.

Rules and the Rule File. The final step in model construction. The rules defined how the numbers in the model go together. These calculation rules, such as

Add line 1 to line 2, save in line 3
Multiply column 6 by 40%, save in column 12
Total cols 1 thru 12, save in col 13
Divide L1 by L2, save L3, cols 1 thru 12,

are helpful in preparing the model for home budgeting.

Report Writer. Allowed the final output to be executed via the printer. (See Fig. 6-57.)

The Planner Plotter in the program provided pictures of the financial situation in the form of bars and graphs (i.e. plotting). In the development of the plot, a graph format was first selected from the following choice of formats: vertical bar graph, horizontal bar graph, point plot, and curve plot.

Note: Vertical and horizontal bar graphs are simply histograms that use the Y and X axis, respectively, to determine the bar height. The point plot places points on the screen according to the values in the data set. The curve plot is similar to the point plot, but goes one step further by connecting the points. (See Fig. 6-58.)

The Planner Plus software program also allows the choice of programming the graphs in any of 16 colors. The graphs illustrated in Fig. 6-54 can be

182

Summary of Assets		SELF	SPOUSE	COMBINED
Cash on hand	(228)	$91616.18	$30233.34	$121849.52
Government securities	(229)	$28512.00	$9408.96	$37920.96
Other securities	(230)	$66166.84	$21835.05	$88001.90
Accounts receivable:				
Relatives & friends	(232)	$20443.10	$6746.22	$27189.32
Others	(233)	$30624.26	$10106.00	$40730.27
Doubtful	(234)	$245029.75	$80859.81	$325889.57
Real estate owned	(235)	$240225.48	$79274.40	$319499.88
R.E. mortgages rec.	(236)	$72149.61	$23809.37	$95958.98
Auto & personal prop.	(237)	$69711.84	$23004.90	$92716.74
Life insurance	(238)	$42397.34	$13991.12	$56388.46
Other assets	(239)	$230552.78	$76082.41	$306635.20
Total Assets	(242)	$647369.71	$213632.00	$861001.71

Fig. 6-57. Financial analysis printout sample.

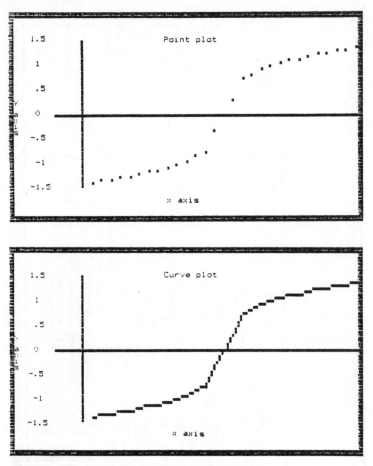

Fig. 6-58. Difference between point plot and curve plot.

executed in any of these colors. As to graphics, the computer system allowed the creation of magnificent graphics by means of its 256 graphic symbols (see Fig. 6-55).

The OSI C8P has 2K of memory dedicated on its model 540 video board, providing a 32 line/64 column format. A graphic character is POKEd to the screen using its code number and the address of the video memory location where it's to be displayed. Using the smaller video memory map as an example (Fig. 6-56), the drawing of a line with the square character no. 161 (refer back to Fig. 6-55) from left to right requires the following programming:

```
10  REM Draw line left to right
20  For X-53699 to 53723
30  POKE x,161
```

40 For T=0 to 20: Next T: REM ---"T" Loop time delay
50 Next x

It is of course possible to move characters (that is, graphic symbols) in an angular motion, rather than straight up and down or left and right. This is achieved by using a FOR-NEXT loop increment other than +32 or −32, or +1/−1. Figure 6-62 illustrates such loop increments.

The telephone interface and modem connected computer communications with the "outside world." Built-into the OSI C8? computer is a Universal Telephone Interface (UTI) which is connected to an FCC-approved CBT DAA (data coupler). The data coupler, in turn, is plugged into the telephone jack of the telephone line.

The UTI allows the computer to pick up the telephone line and dial any number, hang up, and redial, if desired. The device also permits the record-

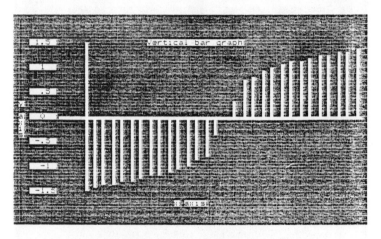

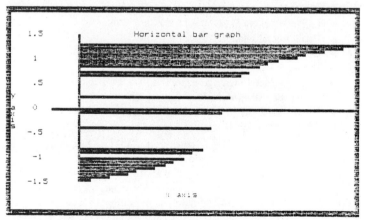

Fig. 6-59. Graph samples.

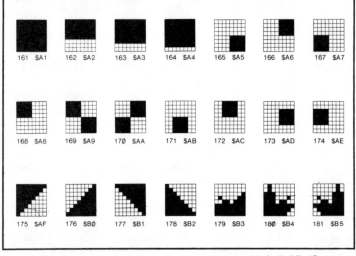

Fig. 6-60. Representative graphic symbols executed with C8P DF. (Courtesy, Ohio Scientific Inc.)

ing of phone messages on a regular cassette recorder. The computer automatically answers the phone when it rings, turns the recorder on, records the message, and turns the recorder off after the caller has hung up. It's also possible to play prerecorded messages via the recorder, just as with a telephone answering machine. And finally, the UTI is equipped with a VOTRAX—a sound synthesizer—that, through a computer-simulated voice, lets the computer talk over the phone line (or over a speaker).

Programming activities consist of:

● Initializing the phone interface.
● Initializing "connect" to the phone line.
● Initiating "disconnect."
● Using the failsafe.
● Computer control of the tape recorder.
● Playing a taped message over the phone line.
● Playing a taped message using the VOTRAX voice synthesizer.
● Automatic dialing/detecting busy signal.
● Originating a call to the modem.
● Automatically answering a call from the modem.

The accompanying software consists of a VOTRAX demo, a phone demo, and a modem use/automatic dial modem.

The use of the VOTRAX voice synthesizer is an intriguing aspect of this computer system. Sixty-three phoneme commands in concert with four voices of inflection provide 252 unique synthesizer inputs, which allow programming the synthesizer in any desired sequential order. The VOTRAX was optimized by OSI for the midwestern, or standard American English,

HEX	DEC								DEC	HEX
		+0	+5	+10	+15	+20	+25	+30		
D000	53248								53279	D01F
D040	53312								53343	D05F
D080	53376								53407	D09F
D0C0	53440								53471	D0DF
D100	53504								53535	D11F
D140	53568								53599	D15F
D180	53632								53663	D19F
D1C0	53696								53727	D1DF
D200	53760								53791	D21F
D240	53824								53855	D25F
D280	53888								53919	D29F
D2C0	53952								53983	D2DF
D300	54016								54047	D31F
D340	54080								54111	D35F
D380	54144								54175	D39F
D3C0	54208								54239	D3DF
D400	54272								54303	D41F
D440	54336								54367	D45F
D480	54400								54431	D49F
D4C0	54464								54495	D4DF
D500	54528								54559	D51F
D540	54592								54623	D55F
D580	54656								54687	D59F
D5C0	54720								54751	D5DF
D600	54784								54815	D61F
D640	54848								54879	D65F
D680	54912								54943	D69F
D6C0	54976								55007	D6DF
D700	55040								55071	D71F
D740	55104								55135	D75F
D780	55168								55199	D79F
D7C0	55232								55263	D7DF
		+0	+5	+10	+15	+20	+25	+30		

Fig. 6-61. Memory graphics map for 32 × 32 format.

187

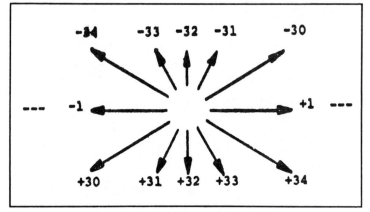

Fig. 6-62. Loop increments for positioning graphic symbols.

dialect, which is the dialect used almost exclusively by the nationwide broadcasting media.

In programming the synthesizer, a number of basic rules had to be considered. For example, the use of consonants had to be carefully spelled out, as shown in Table 6-2.

There are two affricates in English. (An affricate is a two-consonant combination with a fricative stop.) The voiced affricate J is programmed D, J, or DT J. The voiced affricate CH is programmed T, CH, or DT CH. All phonemes in English fall into seven categories, as follows:

Voiced, including all vowels and diphthongs of vowels (A,E,I,U,O,AW,EH,ER,UH,AE,Y,I,AH,OO and OI,OY,OU,OW diphthongs) and the liquid consonants (R,L,W,Y1).

Table 6-2. Programming Consonants with VOTRAX Synthesizer

Consonant	Typical Usage	Consonant	Typical Usage
TH	three	K	key, sick, car
THV	then (voiced TH)	L	lie, well
W	won	NG	bring
R	area	Z	zero
T	tea	SH	shy
P	pot	CH	match, chair (CH is T, CH, or DT)
Y1	yes	V	seven
S	see	B	bob
D	day	N	nine
F	fire	M	my
G	get (the G in gold, not in George)	ZH	azure (the Z)
H	hay, ahead	DT	butter (DT is a tongue flap)
J	jet, George		

Voiced stops (B,D,G)
Nasal closures (M,N,NG)
Unvoiced, including fricatives (S,SH,F,TH) and aspirant H.
Voiced fricatives (Z,ZH,V,THV)
Fricative.stops (T,P,K)
Affricates, including voiced J and unvoiced CH.

Several points of interest should be mentioned here. For example, the letter combination NG doesn't necessarily call for the NG phoneme. This is true if the N forms the end of one syllable and the G forms the beginning of the next, as in the word *engage*. (The N and G are sounded separately.) Thus, in this case, NG was programmed N, G. In the word FINGER, on the other hand, the NG was programmed as either N, G or as NG, G.

In the word *thank*, the N can programmed as N or NG. The A in *thank* is halfway between A and AE, and is perhaps best programmed as AE1, I3—a classical example of an aliphone.

An aliphone is a variation of a basic phoneme. All phonemes in speech context are modified by their phonetic "environment"—that is, whatever is going on before and after the phoneme affects its characteristics (duration, amplitude, frequency components, etc.). This effect is sometimes referred to as the dynamic continuum of which speech is made. A phoneme is merely an operator on the human acoustic output, an operator that, in turn, gets operated upon.

To produce intelligible synthetic speech, the proper aliphone must be generated, and this is done automatically in the VOTRAX. Another example of aliphones is the numerous forms of K - the K in *key*, the K in *look*, and the K sound in Q (which is programmed K,W, as in Quit).

A particular class of phonemes, the liquids R, L, W, and Yl, depend largely on the transitions into and out of these sounds for their recognition. These transitions, important as they are, depend to a great extent on dialect. It was therefore necessary for this programmer to insert transitional phonemes around these sounds in some cases to maximize naturalness and intelligibility.

Inflection was extremely important to avoid a machine-like quality in the VOTRAX speech. Although ideal inflection is a subjective matter, of course, a few simple rules made the programming job easy. The VOTRAX had the capability of having its inflection under computer and software control. This allowed this user to assemble a sentence out of a pre-stored vocabulary of words, and to have these words inflected according to sentence grammar.

The synthesizer was also designed to generate continuous speech, which meant that the words in a sentence had little or no gap in between. The speech was acceptable, if somewhat choppy; it was highly intelligible, however.

The OSI DAC music system is a unique feature for generating music. Two software discs accompanied the computer system; their routines generated signals at the DAC output port that were fed into an auxiliary input jack of an audio amplifier. With the software on these discs, notes and chords were played directly from the keyboard and songs were entered with single or multiple parts. Both discs provided detailed instructions at each step, and required no outside instruction.

Disc number 1 contained software that allowed easy utilization of the DAC converter built into the computer system to generate music. When the disc was run, a description of the contents was displayed on the screen, as shown in Fig. 6-63.

The first two items on the disc—DEMONSTRATION NUMBER 1 and DEMONSTRATION NUMBER 2—were included to demonstrate the single- and multiple-note capabilities of the DAC music system. In specifying either of the two selections, one of two responses was displayed on the screen (Fig. 6-64). These two demonstration programs required no action on the part of this user, other than depressing the carriage return key after reading the description of the program.

The third and fourth items on the disc—KEYBOARD NOTES and KEYBOARD ORGAN—were programs that allowed playing notes or chords using selected keys on the keyboard. Each of these programs printed detailed instructions on the monitor, including a short sequence of key-strokes that played an easily recognized selection. The display of the contents could be restored to the screen from either of these programs by releasing and relocking the shift lock key.

After selecting KEYBOARD NOTES, a selection of voicings was offered and the text shown in Fig. 6-65 was displayed on the screen. If KEYBOARD CHORDS had been selected, the selection of voicings shown in Fig. 6-66 would have appeared.

The last item on disc number 1 was a program called MUSIC BOX. This program allowed this user to enter, store, and play the melodies of up to five songs. When this option was selected, the text shown in Fig. 6-67 appeared on the screen.

As indicated, I had a choice of playing previously entered songs, inputting new songs, reviewing and modifying previously entered songs, or deleting previously entered songs. The entry OPEN indicated that space was available to store an additional song. After selecting OPTION NUMBER 1, the computer responded: WHICH SELECTION DO YOU WISH TO PLAY? When the selection entered finished playing, the computer returned the program to MUSIC BOX. Then, after selecting OPTION NUMBER 2, the computer searched the list of titles to find the first open entry, and responded as shown in Fig. 6-68.

The title of the new song—"My Bonnie Lies over the Ocean"—was entered. The computer accepted the title and printed the detailed instructions shown in Fig. 6-64. According to program instructions, notes were entered that were checked by the computer for name, octave, and length for validity. Changes and modifications could be made. (The programming guide conveniently assisted these activities.)

190

```
OHIO SCIENTIFIC DAC MUSIC SYSTEM -- DISK NUMBER ONE
SEPTEMBER 1979

THIS IS DISK NUMBER ONE OF THE OHIO SCIENTIFIC D/A MUSIC
SYSTEM.  THIS DISK OFFERS THE FOLLOWING OPTIONS --

1   DEMONSTRATION NUMBER 1 -- FRERE JACQUES
2   DEMONSTRATION NUMBER 2 -- SILENT NIGHT
3   KEYBOARD NOTES -- PLAYS SINGLE NOTES FROM THE KEYBOARD
4   KEYBOARD ORGAN -- PLAYS CHORDS FROM THE KEYBOARD
5.  MUSIC BOX -- ALLOWS ENTRY AND PLAYBACK OF MUSICAL
                 SELECTIONS WITH ONE PART

DISK NUMBER TWO CONTAINS A PACKAGE OF PROGRAMS WHICH ALLOW
THE USER TO ENTER, STORE, EDIT AND PLAYBACK COMPLEX MUSICAL
SELECTIONS WITH FOUR MUSICAL PARTS

WHICH OF THE ABOVE OPTIONS DO YOU WISH TO USE?
```

Fig. 6-63. Display, OSI DAC music system. (Courtesy, Ohio Scientific Inc.)

(DEMONSTRATION NUMBER 1)

THE OHIO SCIENTIFIC DAC MUSIC SYSTEM CAN PLAY MUSICAL
SELECTIONS WITH UP TO FOUR DISTINCT MUSICAL PARTS. THE
FOLLOWING VERSION OF FRERE JACQUES ILLUSTRATES BOTH THE
SINGLE AND MULTIPLE PART CAPABILITIES. THE ENTIRE
SELECTION IS PLAYED FIRST WITH A SINGLE PART. IT IS THEN
REPEATED WITH ADDITIONAL PARTS BEING ADDED UNTIL FOUR
DISTINCT PARTS ARE PLAYING SIMULTANEOUSLY. FINALLY THE
PARTS DROP OFF ONE-BY-ONE UNTIL A SINGLE PART IS LEFT.
DEPRESS THE CARRIAGE RETURN TO BEGIN PLAYING THE SELECTION.

(DEMONSTRATION NUMBER 2)

THE OHIO SCIENTIFIC DAC MUSIC SYSTEM CAN PLAY MUSICAL
SELECTIONS WITH UP TO FOUR DISTINCT MUSICAL PARTS.
IN ADDITION TO ALLOWING THE USER TO PLAY ROUNDS SUCH AS
ON DEMONSTRATION NUMBER 1, THIS CAPABILITY ALLOWS THE
USER TO ENTER CHORDS WHEN PLAYING A SONG. AS AN
EXAMPLE THE FOLLOWING SELECTION WILL FIRST BE PLAYED WITH
SINGLE NOTES AND THEN IN FOUR FULL PARTS. DEPRESS THE
CARRIAGE RETURN TO PLAY THE SELECTION.

Fig. 6-64. Demonstration program for OSI DAC music system. (Courtesy, Ohio Scientific Inc.)

THE COMPUTER WILL ALLOW YOU TO PLAY NOTES IN THREE OCTAVES
BY ENTERING THE NOTES THROUGH THE KEYBOARD. THE THREE OCTAVES
ARE THE OCTAVE FROM MIDDLE-C TO HIGH-C AND THE OCTAVES
IMMEDIATELY ABOVE AND BELOW THIS OCTAVE

TO PLAY A NOTE ENTER ANY OF THE FOLLOWING NOTE NAMES---

A,A+ OR B-,B,C,C+ OR D-,D,D+ OR E-,E,F,F+ OR G-,G,G+ OR A-

THE NOTE PLAYED WILL BE THE NOTE NAMED IN THE MIDDLE OCTAVE
UNLESS YOU SIMULTANEOUSLY DEPRESS THE 1 OR 2 KEY.

    1   SELECTS THE LOWER OCTAVE
    2   SELECTS THE UPPER OCTAVE

AS AN EXAMPLE THE FOLLOWING SEQUENCE OF NOTES PLAYS THE
BALLAD AMAZING GRACE

G1 C E D E E D C A1 G1 G1 D E D E
D   G G G E D E E D C A1 G1 G1 C
E   D E D C

TO TERMINATE THE PROGRAM RELEASE AND RELOCK THE SHIFT LOCK KEY

Fig. 6-65. Screen display, OSI DAC music system. (Courtesy, Ohio Scientific Inc.)

CHORDS ARE COMBINATIONS OF THREE OR MORE NOTES PLAYED AT THE
SAME TIME. MANY MUSIC BOOKS LIST BOTH THE MELODY AND CHORDS TO
ACCOMPANY THE MELODY. WITH THIS PROGRAM YOU CAN PLAY CHORDS
TO ACCOMPANY SONGS IN A GUITAR STYLE.

TWELVE GROUPS OF CHORDS ARE AVAILABLE. THE GROUPS ARE
IDENTIFIED BY THE FOLLOWING NOTE NAMES--

A,A+ OR B-,B,C,C+ OR D-,D,D+ OR E-,E,F,F+ OR G-,G,G+ OR A-

BY DEPRESSING THE KEY(S) OF EACH NOTE NAME YOU CAN PLAY THE
FIRST CHORD (THE MAJOR CHORD) IN EACH GROUP. THE OTHER FIVE
CHORDS IN EACH GROUP ARE PLAYED BY DEPRESSING THE 1,2,3,4 OR 5
KEY TOGETHER WITH THE NOTE NAME. THE CHORDS OBTAINED ARE

1=DOM 7   2=MINOR   3=MINOR 7   4=AUG   5=DIM

PLAYED WITH THE CORRECT TEMPO THE FOLLOWING SEQUENCE OF CHORDS
PLAYS I'VE BEEN WORKING ON THE RAILROAD

G (8X) , C (4X) , G (10X) , A1 (4X), D1 (7X) , G (2X)
C (5X) , A3 (2X) , B1 (1X) , C (6X), G (4X) , D1 (2X) , G (1X)

TO TERMINATE THE PROGRAM RELEASE AND RELOCK THE SHIFT LOCK KEY

Fig. 6-66. Screen display of KEYBOARD CHORDS had been selected. (Courtesy, Ohio Scientific Inc.)

THIS PROGRAM ALLOWS YOU TO ENTER, STORE AND PLAY THE
MELODIES OF UP TO 5 SONGS. THE FOLLOWING SELECTIONS
ARE CURRENTLY AVAILABLE---

SELECTION   TITLE
1   MORNING HAS BROKEN
2   LET THERE BE PEACE ON EARTH
3   WHAT A WONDERFUL WORLD
4   I WALK THE LINE
5   OKIE FROM MUSKOGEE

YOU HAVE THE FOLLOWING OPTIONS---

1   PLAY AN EXISTING SONG
2   INPUT A NEW SONG
3   REVIEW/MODIFY AN EXISTING SONG
4   DELETE AN EXISTING SONG
5   QUIT

WHICH OPTION DO YOU WISH TO UTILIZE?

Fig. 6-67. Screen display, OSI DAC music system. (Courtesy, Ohio Scientific Inc.)

```
THE NEW SELECTION WILL BE SELECTION
NUMBER 07

THE TITLE OF THE NEW SELECTION CAN BE
UP TO 30 CHARACTERS LONG.  INPUT THE
TITLE OF THE NEW SELECTION ?
```

Fig. 6-68. Screen display, OSI DAC music system. (Courtesy, Ohio Security Inc.)

Disc number 2 of the DAC program contained an advanced version of the program MUSIC BOX. The major enhancements offered were:

● Storage for 10 selections.
● Ability to play four-part music.
● Ability to specify the voicings (waveforms) for each of the four parts.
● Ability to modify the tempo of a selection.
● Ability to add to a selection previously entered.

After inserting this disc in the disc drive, the statement ***PREPARING TO RUN MUSIC PROGRAM*** appeared on the screen. After a brief delay during which the computer read the disc file with the names of the selections stored, screen display the text shown in Fig. 6-70.

Again, this user went through extensive programming sequences for each option. This system certainly offered excellent opportunities for using the computer as a musical instrument.

One of the most valuable aspects of the OSI C8P computer system was utilization of the HOME CONTROL AND SECURITY PROGRAM. Without having to run any wires, the computer operated lamps and small appliances when connected through the home-control system—the BSR X-10, a remote ac signaling system. The computer activated this command console, which, in turn, sent a signal over the home wiring. The system was sensed at the appropriate device by a small switch module plugged into the ac outlet.

To run this ac control program, the software supplied was utilized and the program written according to my plan—i.e., certain lights to be turned on at 6:00 PM, others at a later time, and the lights to be turned off at different times in the morning. Here's how it works.

The house-code dial on the command console (1, in Fig. 6-76) selects one of 16 letters, providing a choice of 16 codes. The keyboard of the unit has 16 keys in Fig. 6-66, each one corresponding to the number set on the code dial of each lamp, as follows:

ON	sends "turn on" command to module selected.
OFF	sends "turn off" command to module selected.
DIM	sends "dim" command to module selected.

196

SONGS ARE LIMITED TO NO MORE THAN 254 NOTES. NOTES ARE
ENTERED IN THE FOLLOWING ORDER -- NAME,OCTAVE,LENGTH

NAME--
   C,D,E,F,G,A,B,C+,D+,F+,G+,A+,D-,E-,G-,A-,B-,R
   + IS FOR SHARP, - IS FOR FLAT, R IS FOR REST
   PRECEDE THE NAME BY > TO TIE IT TO THE PRECEDING NOTE
OCTAVE--
   -3,-2,-1,0,1,2,3
   THE OCTAVE FROM MIDDLE C TO HIGH C IS NUMBERED 0
   OTHER OCTAVES ARE NUMBERED ABOVE AND BELOW THIS OCTAVE
LENGTH--USUALLY A MULTIPLE OF 0.25 LESS THAN OR EQUAL TO 4
   .25=1/16 NOTE   .5=1/8 NOTE   1=1/4 NOTE   2=1/2 NOTE
   4=WHOLE NOTE   ADD HALF VALUE SHOWN FOR A DOTTED NOTE
ENTER   END,0,0   TO SIGNAL THE END OF THE SONG

EXAMPLES--
   D-,-1,1   1/4 NOTE, D FLAT, OCTAVE ABOVE MIDDLE OCTAVE
   >B,0,.5   1/8 NOTE, B, MIDDLE OCTAVE, TIED TO
                PRECEDING NOTE
   R,0,4   REST FOR A WHOLE NOTE
   END,0,0   THE END OF THE SONG

Fig. 6-69. Screen display, OSI DAC music system. (Courtesy, Ohio Scientific Inc.)

197

```
THIS PROGRAM PLAYS MUSICAL SELECTIONS IN FOUR PARTS
THE FOLLOWING SELECTIONS ARE AVAILABLE--
SELECTION              TITLE                        TEMPO
  1        FRERE JACQUES                              2
  2        SILENT NIGHT HOLY NIGHT                    3
  3        JESU JOY OF MAN'S DESIRING                 3
  4        DELTA DAWN                                 2
  5        STAR WARS-MAIN TITLE                       2
  6        STAR WARS-CANTINA BAND                     1
  7        PRELUDE IN C MIN -- J S BACH               2
  8        (OPEN)                                     0
  9        (OPEN)                                     0
 10        (OPEN)                                     0

YOU HAVE THE FOLLOWING OPTIONS--

  1  PLAY A SONG
  2  INPUT A SONG
  3  REVIEW/MODIFY A SONG
  4  DELETE AN EXISTING SONG
  5  ADD TO A SONG

WHICH OPTION DO YOU WISH TO UTILIZE?
```

Fig. 6-70. Screen display, OSI DAC music system. (Courtesy, Ohio Scientific Inc.)

BRIGHT   sends "brighten" command to module selected.

ALL LIGHTS sends "turn on" command to all controlled lamps.
ON

ALL OFF   sends "turn off" command to every controlled module.

The lamp module has two dials—a house-code dial corresponding to the house-code dial of the console, and a unit code dial with 16 possible settings, corresponding to the command keys of the console. (See Fig. 6-67.)

The setup is done as follows. (Refer back to Fig. 6-72.)

● Set house-code dial on command console to "A."
● Plug command console into 110-volt outlet.
● Set house-code dial on module to "A."
● Set black unit code dial on module to "2."
● Plug lamp into lamp cord receptacle of lamp module.
● Plug lamp module into 110-volt outlet.
● Turn regular lamp on/off switch to On until lamp goes on.

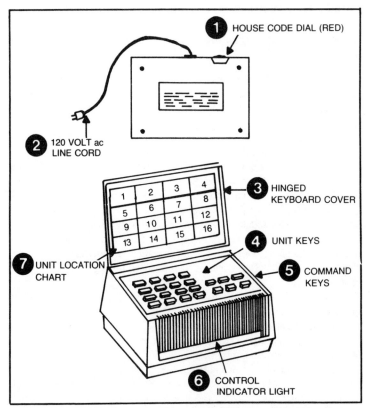

Fig. 6-71. Command console for light control. (Courtesy, Ohio Scientific Inc.)

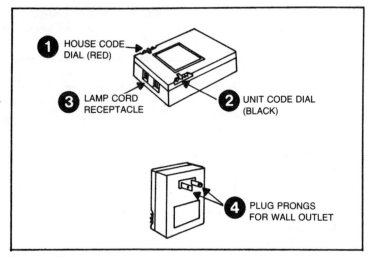

Fig. 6-72. Dial controls of lamp module. (Courtesy, Ohio Scientific Inc.)

● Press command key 2 on console and then OFF key. Lamp will go out.

In the same fashion, lamps can be controlled for "dim" (and more than one lamp controlled from the console). Small appliances such as fans and radios can also be controlled by means of the appliance module and the command console.

The home-security devices provide for checking for both fire and intruders. All alarms report their status by radio control to the home-security command module connected to the computer system. Each alarm module contains a sensor, battery power, and a radio transmitter to assure reliable and tamper-resistant operation. The fire alarm senses temperature (thermal contact) or smoke (ionization detector). The intruder alarms are silent, magnetically actuated door- or window-position sensors. By combining these alarms with computerized response, critical situations can be managed. The alarms were located at the computer address 63232 and the alarm control at 63233. The alarms were enabled through various program sequences.

Following is a description (and a review of some of the installation procedures) of the security system.

The receiver is a tabletop unit (Fig. 6-73) powered by 110 volts. (A 12-V battery pack can provide backup power.) The unit has four basic types of alarm: fire, intrusion, emergency, and maintenance. When an alarm occurs, the receiver provides both audible and visual signals to indicate the nature of it. The TEST/INTRUSION OFF switch has these states and associated functions: NORMAL—all controls and indicators functioning normally; TEST—receiver being tested (by pressing this switch); and

INTRUSION OFF—system turns off during daytime to allow normal entry and exit of the occupants of the house.

The door-intrusion unit consists of one magnetic switch, which is mounted on the door as close to the edge as possible (C in Fig. 6-74); a magnet mounted on the door frame as close as possible to the magnetic switch (D) and then connected to the transmitter by means of two wires. The transmitter operates on a 9-V battery and can be locked two ways: with a permanent lock key (1 in Fig. 6-74(E)), or with a removable key that can be carried on a key chain (2 in Fig. 6-74(E)).

The window-intrusion system consists of the same components, but a slider is provided to allow opening the window for ventilation without disrupting the alarm operation (Fig. 6-75). Without this bracket, the window-intrusion system can be used for various types of windows (Fig. 6-75(C)).

The smoke detector, which operates on a 9-V battery, also works on the radio transmitting system, sending a signal to the receiver when smoke enters the unit or when the temperature reaches a certain maximum.

Since both the fire and intrusion transmitters and the tabletop receiver work on the principle of radio waves (maximum range 200 feet), the units are designed to operate on 16 different transmission/receiving codes. The code set by the manufacturer is "1" (see Fig. 6-76). Changing the codes is accomplished by cutting certain wires (which should only be done in the unlikely event that a neighbor has the same system and operates on the same code as you do). The manufacturer suggests that a minimum number of wires should be cut. (Codes 2, 3, 5, and 9 require the cutting of only one wire.)

Summary, OSI C8P DF

Although I didn't use the computer system to its fullest, the possibilities of running programs on the Ohio Scientific C8P DF—or on any other computer—strike me as almost endless.

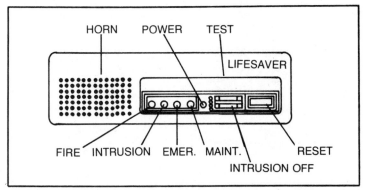

Fig. 6-73. Receiver console of security system. (Courtesy, Ohio Scientific Inc.)

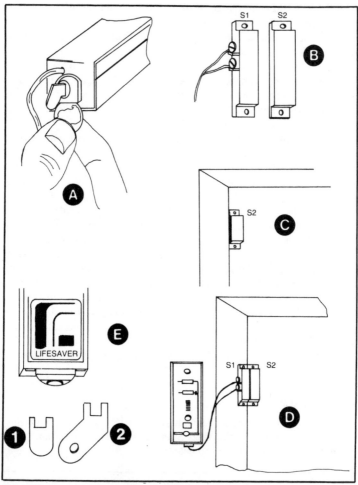

Fig. 6-74. Door intrusion system installation.

In the November, 1980 issue of *Interface Age*, William J. Spitz discussed a program designed to audit heat loss in the home. He describes the purpose of his audit program as being "to pin down the location and amount of energy lost from a house. The objectives are to categorize all the surfaces through which heat energy passes out to the environment, and determine the rates at which energy flows through a particular surface. Taken step by step, the audit is a straightforward process that will really give an accurate thermal profile."

He designed a questionnaire that the homeowner could use as a guide when inspecting his house. A complete program listing is included with the article. After reading it, there would seem to be no way for anybody to audit

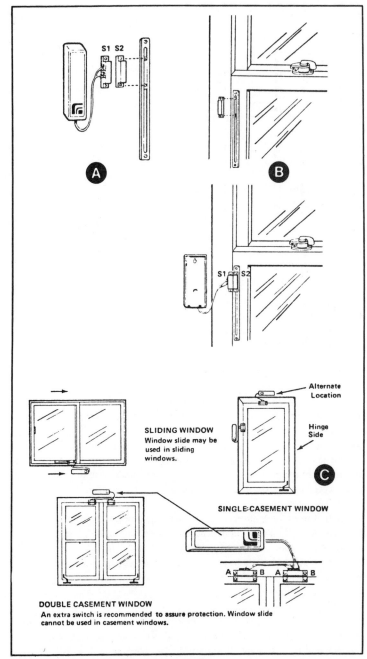

Fig. 6-75. Window-intrusion system installation.

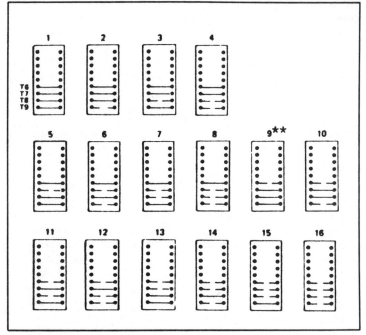

Fig. 6-76. Code chart of security system.

the loss of home energy anywhere near as accurate or as fast as with the aid of a home computer.

Another project that came to my attention was a computer-aided design of handweaving. Mr. and Mrs. Tom Windeknecht use a computer system to accomplish a faster draft operation in the design of weaving patterns. Since weaving patterns must usually be generated by hand on graph paper—a tedious and time-consuming effort—the use of a computer has aided Mrs. Windeknecht tremendously in the graphics technique of drafting. The computer system consists of a KIM-1 processor, Ohio Scientific 440B video board, TV typewriter, cassette recorder, and 8K bytes of external memory. The activities of the Windeknechts have culminated in the writing of a book. Although Mrs. Windeknecht indicated that the programming and the design of the mechanism of a weaving draft is not for beginners, it serves to illustrate that a home computer's use is limited only by the user's imagination.

QUASAR

In this writer's opinion, the culmination of the use of home computers is the portable computer system by Quasar. This portable, briefcase system (shown in Fig. 6-82) works either on batteries or 110-V ac power. It consists of the following modules:

- 6502 microprocessor system with display (full dot matrix, LCD, 159 columns of 8 dots each); keyboard (65 keys, alphanumeric and special-function) and memory (4K bytes built-in, maximum 1.6K ROM).
- Microprinter.
- Cassette adapter (allowing two cassette recorders to be connected).
- Capsule extender (allows four more modules capsules of memory to be added to the computer's three modules) the computer holds three memory modules.
- Programmable memory module (allows 4K bytes of RAM).

PANASONIC

Another unit recently introduced but not available at the time of this writing is Panasonic's HHC (Hand-Held Computer)—the third such device, after Radio Shack's and Sinclair's introductions.

As an "introduction to computerism" the unit may well become very popular. It has a full complement of keys, and a built-in liquid-crystal, one-line display (24 characters, upper- and lowercase dot-matrix). It also has the capability to be connected to a host of peripherals. RAM expansion units and an acoustic coupler are being planned.

Built around a 6502 microprocessor, it has 2K RAM memory and four slots for ROM cartridges. Other points include the following:

- 44-pin expander that allows connections peripheral such as a portable 16-character-line thermal printer; ROM extender that adds up to four program-data cartridges; RAM expander; modem; cassette recorder interface; and color television interface allowing 16 lines by 24 characters, and 48 times 64 pixels.
- 2K RAM is internally expandable to 4K and 16K bytes of ROM.
- Total RAM/ROM expansion to 4 megabytes.
- 65-button keyboard.

PERSONAL MICRO COMPUTERS

The PMC-80 contains a CPU, I/O devices, and a mass-storage device—the Z-80, a keyboard, video interface, and built-in cassette recorder. There are two versions, one with 16K RAM memory and one with 4K RAM. The video interface (with rf modulator) lets you connect the computer to a television set or monitor. The operating system is BASIC. (See Fig. 6-77.)

An optional S-100 bus expansion unit allows you to attach a number of peripherals and accessories (Fig. 6-78). The system is ready to operate immediately after unpacking and the necessary connections are made (Fig. 6-79).

The unit, called Video Genie System, allows two kinds of display formats; 64 characters per line or 32 characters per line. The keyboard (Fig. 6-80) has 10 special function keys:

Fig. 6-77. PMC-80 personal/home computer. (Courtesy, Personal Micro Computer.)

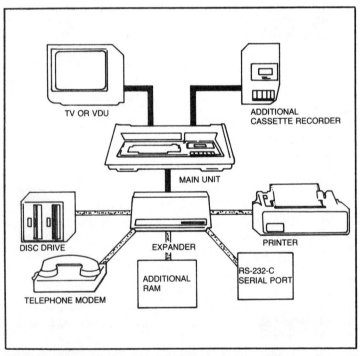

Fig. 6-78. Expansion system of the PMC-80 computer. (Courtesy, Personal Micro Computer.)

● PAGE (selects page for display).

● FI (isolates cassette from the control of the computer during winding and rewinding operations, and allows manual cassette motor control).

● BREAK (breaks a running program and a return to the active command level).

● NEWLINE (enters a line of command or data into the computer).

● BACKSPACE (cancels the character previously typed).

● ESC (escape command).

● CTL (moves the cursor to the beginning of the next line).

● SHIFT/CTL/I (tab function, moves the cursor eight spaces to the right).

● SHIFT/CTL/Y (same as print).

● SHIFT/BACKSPACE - deletes a line.

The cassette recorder is a high-fidelity audio recorder with six piano keys and a three-digit counter. It functions as a regular audio recorder. If programs require additional storage, a second cassette recorder can be connected through an output jack on the computer (Fig. 6-81).

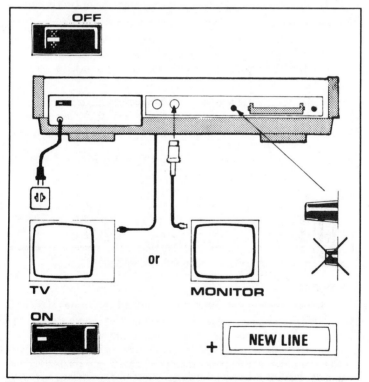

Fig. 6-79. Easy connections of PMC-80. (Courtesy, Personal Micro Computer.)

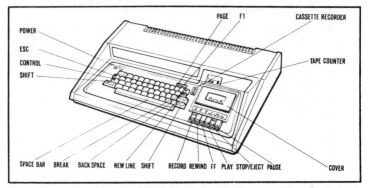

Fig. 6-80. Keyboard layout of PMC-80. (Courtesy, Personal Micro Computer.)

Designed to emulate the Radio Shack TRS-80 Model I, all software available for the TRS-80 operates on the PMC-80. With the PMC expander, all peripherals designed for the TRS-80, including disc drives, printers, speech-recognition devices, modems, and the like, will connect to the PMC-80. These peripherals are discussed in more detail later on in this book.

● TV adapter (allows connection of the system to a TV monitor).

● I/O Adapter (allows connection of six peripherals to the system).

● Modem (provides two-way communications through the telephone lines).

All components mentioned above fit into a briefcase, making it the only system today that you can carry back and forth with you wherever you go. Such ease and simplicity have a lot to recommend them when it comes to choosing a home computer.

Note: At the time of this writing, this computer system wasn't yet ready for delivery, so further details were unavailable.

RADIO SHACK

Radio Shack manufactures six different computer systems: TRS-80I, TRS-80II, TRS-80III, TRS-80C, TRS-80HHC, TRS-80 Videotex. (See Fig. 6-83.) The Model I is no longer manufactured, but the company continues to support the line with parts, accessories, and related materials.

TRS-80 Model I

There are still many of these units in the field, and you may be able to obtain one from a computer user who is upgrading to a more sophisticated computer. There are two levels of the Model I. Level I and Level II. The difference is that the Level II has disc capability; availability of 12K ROM (vs. 4K ROM for Level I); numeric accuracy of 16 digits (instead of 6); 94 BASIC commands (rather than 34 for Level I); more error codes; and faster cassette speed.

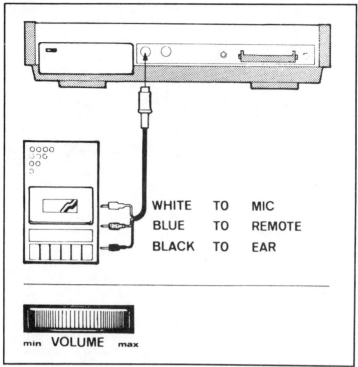

WHITE   TO   MIC
BLUE   TO   REMOTE
BLACK   TO   EAR

min VOLUME max

Fig. 6-81. Connecting additional cassette recorder to PMC-80. (Courtesy, Personal Micro Computer.)

Fig. 6-82. Portable, hand-held computer system. (Courtesy, Quasar.)

Fig. 6-83. TRS-80 personal computers from Radio Shack. *Left*: TRS-80 Color Computer with monitor; *Right*: TRS-80 Model III; *Center*: Hand Held Pocket Computer. (Courtesy, Radio Shack.)

Both levels of the Model I are self-contained computers with built-in 12-in. video display monitor; 53-key keyboard, and the capability to expand by means of an expansion unit for integral connections to a printer; up to four floppy discs; two cassette recorders; RS-232C serial interface; and plug-in sockets to expand the memory to 16K or 32K bytes.

Extensive software programs are available for the Model I, and support items include:

● Telephone Interface II (an acoustic coupler that lets you communicate with other computer users and access such time-sharing organizations as CompuServe and The Source).

● Direct-connect modem (interfaces between the computer and the telephone handset).

● Plug 'n Power controller (connects to the cassette port of the computer and sends the computer's commands through the ac electrical system to remote modules; controls up to 256 lights and appliances automatically).

● Expansion Interface (allows you to add up to 32K additional RAM storage, plus four mini-disc drives; printer; dual cassette recorder; and RS-232C interface card for communications purposes).

● Voxbox (lets you speak into a microphone and program the computer through verbal commands to respond to simple words).

● Model I Mini-Disc Drives (lets you connect up to four drives to the computer).

● Voice Synthesizer (adds the capability of simulated speech, under program control).

• BASIC Programming Software (a teaching program to introduce BASIC; see Fig. 6-84).

• Telephone Linkage System (a modem that connects easily and simply to the Model I; see Fig. 6-85).

Available from Emtrol Systems, the modem unit interfaces between the computer and the telephone system in half or full duplex; no expansion interface is required. It provides the connection with either CompuServe or The Source. By placing the telephone on top of the modem, easy access as well as space-saving is afforded (see Fig. 6-86).

TRS-80 Model II

Although the Model II (Fig. 6-87) is by no means cheap and is designed basically for business use, it's still classified as a personal computer. It's contained in one compact, desktop cabinet that includes a built-in 8-in.

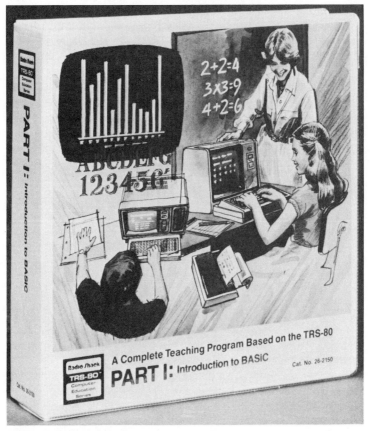

Fig. 6-84. Software program for teaching BASIC computer language. (Courtesy, Radio Shack.)

211

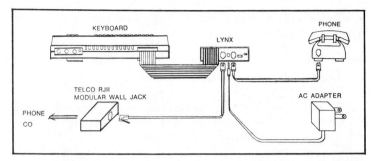

Fig. 6-85. Easy connection and interface of modem and TRS-80 Model I computer.

floppy-disc drive; a high-resolution 12-in. video display; and a detachable keyboard with 76 alphanumeric and special-entry keys. The display screen will display 24 lines of upper- and lowercase characters.

There are two versions of the Model II—one with 32K RAM and one with 64K RAM. The disc drive provides 416K bytes of memory, and—by plugging in a disc-expansion unit—you can add three more drives, providing a total of 2 megabytes of memory.

There are two serial I/O ports and one parallel I/O port, allowing you to add printers, plotters, digitizers, and modems. Software programs available

Fig. 6-86. Modem (telephone interface) for Model I TRS-80 computer. (Courtesy, Emtrol Systems.)

from Radio Shack are basically business-oriented, but other vendors offer a variety of programs in a number of fields.

TRS-80 Model III

The Model III (Fig. 6-88) is a well-planned improvement on the Model I. It's a totally self-contained unit (no detachable keyboard) with a 65-key keyboard; 12-key datapad; 12-in. built-in high-resolution B/W monitor; and the capability of adding two internal double-density floppy-disc drives.

You can purchase a very basic Model III with 4K RAM memory and 4K of ROM, but without the disc drives. Then, you can build up—that is, add 16K of RAM and 10K of ROM. (The latter allows, upper- and lowercase characters; the basic unit has only uppercase characters). You can also add BASIC III. (The basic unit allows BASIC Level I only.) Finally, the additional ROM memory permits two-speed cassette operation.

The modular design of the Model III provides you with the opportunity to upgrade to 48K of RAM; to add two internal double-density floppy-disc drives; and to add two more floppy-disc drives externally. So the top of the line offers you 48K RAM, 14K ROM, and 670K additional programmable/ usable memory, plus RS-232C interface.

The keyboard of the Model III is identical to that of the Model I, providing 96 text characters, 64 graphics characters (see Fig. 6-89), and 160 special characters. And, since the software between the Model I and Model III is compatible, many programs are available.

Available additional hardware includes:

● Microconnection (from Microperipherals Corp.) (permits the Model III to communicate with other computers and time-sharing organizations; see Fig. 6 -90).

Fig. 6-87. TRS-80 Model II microcomputer. (Courtesy, Radio Shack.)

Fig. 6-88. TRS-80 Model III computer. (Courtesy, Radio Shack.)

● Smart III (a program that permits off-line text preparation, again from Microperipherals Corp).

● K-8 Math Cross Reference (an educational resource program from Radio Shack to teach children mathematical instructions; see Fig. 6-91).

● The Whistler (from Small Systems Software; see Fig. 6-92). This device plugs in to the tape-recorder output of the computer. With an ultrasonic oscillator and piezoelectric transducer, the unit sends an ultrasonic signal to the BSR Home Control System (available at Sears and other stores) to control the lights and appliances in your home. With the software furnished you can program the computer for the exact time periods you want electrical appliances and/or lights go on or off.

TRS-80C Color Computer

For the price—of approximately $400—this is one of the most interesting and exciting home-computer devices ever introduced in the marketplace. The unit (see Fig. 6-93) comes complete with 53-key standard keyboard, 8K BASIC ROM, 4K RAM, eight colors and sound, two joystick interfaces, high-speed cassette interface, and an RS-232C serial interface—all in a single enclosure. Included with the unit is Level I BASIC, sufficient to run on the 4K RAM.

From here on you can build the unit up by adding one or more of the following:

● Program Paks (plug into the side of the machine; such software programs as Personal Finance, Bingo Math, Music, and games: Quasar Commander, Football, Checkers, Chess, Pinball).

- 16K RAM expansion with Extended Color BASIC.
- Color video receiver (display provides 16 lines by 31 characters, 32 × 64 pixels with eight colors or 128 × 192 for four colors. Colors are green, yellow, blue, red, buff, cyan, magenta, and orange.
- Cassette recorder (stores and saves additional programs).
- Joysticks (add excitement to games, and lets you maneuver on-screen objects and graphics).

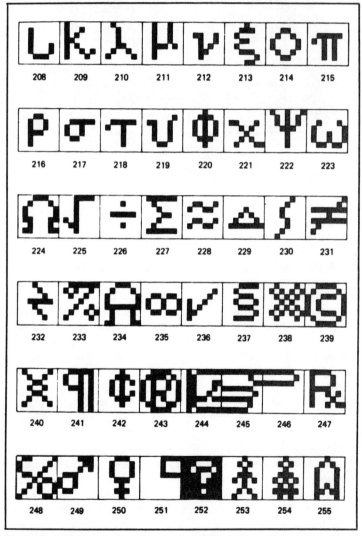

Fig. 6-89. Sixty-four graphics characters of TRS-80 Model III computer. (Courtesy, Radio Shack.)

Fig. 6-90. Microconnection modem for TRS-80 Model III computer. (Courtesy, Microperipherals Corp.)

● Line printer (allows you to print high-density graphics, similar in quality to the ones appearing on the display).

● Quick printer (mini-line printer for printing text).

● Modem I (for transferring data from one location to another).

For those who need more storage capacity, Radio Shack is planning to introduce a floppy-disc system for the color computer.

Different from their other computers, Radio Shack's color computer is built around the Motorola MC6809E microprocessor. One of the advantages of this system is that another chip—the SAM (Synchronous Address Multiplexer)—provides the services previously handled by the Z-80, such as memory refresh, address selection, and data transfer. This gives the color computer a number of powerful features: different video modes and different screen size, to mention two. Figure 6-94 shows a block diagram of the color computer.

TRS-80 Pocket Computer

This small, almost hand-size computer (Fig. 6-95) may perhaps be the best introduction to computing for someone who's never operated a real computer before. Data are displayed on a dot-matrix liquid-crystal screen that shows a single line of up to 24 characters. You execute data input through the 53-key alphanumeric keyboard. The keyboard arrangement includes 37 keys for alphabetic input and special functions, most having a dual function when used with the SHIFT key, plus a 20-key section for numeric input, numeric functions mode, and editing. Memory consists of 11K ROM and 1.9K RAM.

You can program this pocket computer to do almost any of the smaller jobs that the TRS-80 microcomputers can do (except those requiring graphics capability). Each program in memory can be identified with a key label and run, simply by pressing the specified key. Programs can accept words and names as data for storage in memory, and can even search for them (after a fashion). You simply switch to the RUN mode to run your program(s) from memory. (Several can be stored at the same time.)

Power comes from four long-life (300 hours) mercury batteries; an automatic power-off feature saves battery life if no entry has been made in seven minutes. Even with the power off, however, programs and data are in permanent memory for instant recall.

Fig. 6-91. Math Cross Reference program for math instructions. (Courtesy, Radio Shack.)

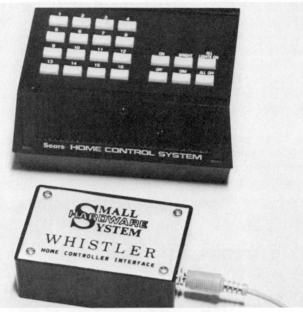

Fig. 6-92. Whistler ultrasonic interface to be used with BSR to control electrical appliances, lights, and similar devices. (Courtesy, Small System Software.)

Fig. 6-93. TRS-80 Color Computer. (Television monitor not included in basic package). (Courtesy, Radio Shack.)

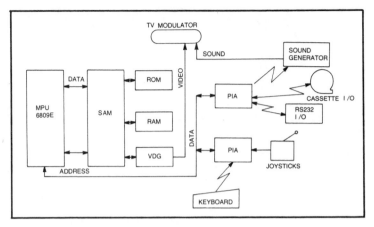

Fig. 6-94. TRS color computer block diagram.

A cassette interface (Fig. 6-96) can be attached to the pocket computer; the interface in turn, connects to a cassette recorder, to enable you to store and save programs. Software programs presently available are Business/Financial, Statistics, Real Estate, Aviation, Civil Engineering, Personal Finance, Games Pack I, and Math Drill. Others should be available soon.

An add-on for the pocket computer recently announced by Radio Shack is a printer/cassette interface. This combined printer/cassette interface comes with long-life batteries, ac adapter/charger, cassette recorder connecting cable, replaceable printer ribbon cartridge, and three rolls of paper. By adding this interface you can make permanent hard copies of your programs. The printer provides a 16-column printout in dot-matrix format, and you don't have to connect cables when interfacing the computer with the

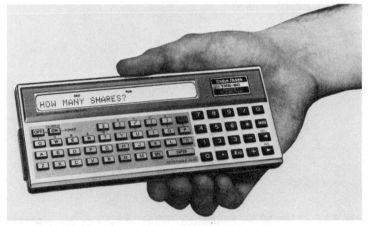

Fig. 6-95. TRS-80 pocket computer. (Courtesy, Radio Shack.)

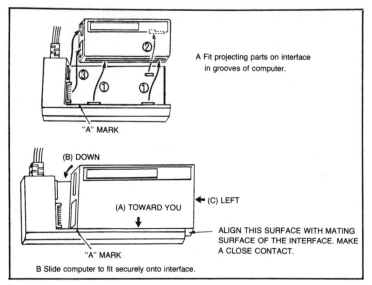

A Fit projecting parts on interface in grooves of computer.

"A" MARK

(B) DOWN

(A) TOWARD YOU ← (C) LEFT

ALIGN THIS SURFACE WITH MATING SURFACE OF THE INTERFACE. MAKE A CLOSE CONTACT.

"A" MARK

B Slide computer to fit securely onto interface.

Fig. 6-96. Installing the pocket computer to the cassette interface. (Courtesy, Radio Shack.)

printer: the pocket computer slides right into the interface for direct connection. (See Fig. 6-97).

Voxbox Speech/Recognition Device

This speech-recognition unit allows you to use words and phrases to control and instruct your computer, and also to enter data. You just focus on the work or play at hand, and watch the video display without the distraction of having to type on the keyboard. The unit connects to the computer.

Fig. 6-97. Printer/cassette interface for TRS-80 pocket computer. (Courtesy, Radio Shack.)

After hardware setup, the applicable software has to be used to install the driver program. This driver program is a machine-language file stored on a cassette and loaded into the highest RAM address in the computer. There are three different machine-language tapes, corresponding to the three possible memory sizes—16K, 32K, and 48K RAM. After certain command modes, the tape will load the computer.

Speaking into the microphone has to be done slowly, consistently, and as distinctly as possible, using as little voice inflection as possible. The vocabulary size of the device is 32 words. You can use any language or words you wish: the display may prompt you in English, but it's not necessary to use the same English word. Once you've trained the voxbox in a given vocabulary pronounce the words consistently, so that the unit can recognize them more reliably.

The Voxbox has three routines you can call from BASIC: *initialization*, which clears the speech files (previously stored speech data is lost); *training*, which accepts known spoken words and extracts features from these words which are stored away for future comparison with unknown words during recognition; and *recognition*, which identifies unknown words spoken to the device. It may be called as frequently as desired after training.

All three routines have to be programmed into the computer.

RCA (SINGLE-BOARD)

The Cosmac VIP

The Cosmac VIP-711 uses a CDP1802 single-chip microprocessor. Four 4K bit static RAM circuits provide 2K of memory, and sockets are provided for an additional 2K. Input is through an integral 16-key hexadecimal keypad; output is through a CDP1861 video circuit that generates graphic displays for your video monitor or television set. Long-term storage is provided by an interface that allows you to store data on a cassette recorder. Built-in sound consists of a fixed-frequency audio-tone generator and speaker controlled by the processor. You can expand the RAM up to 4K.

When you receive the unit, it looks much as shown in Fig. 6-98; after you've made all the connections, the installation should look like the illustration in Fig. 6-99.

To write a program for the Cosmac VIP, you have to learn either CHIP-8 (VIP's user-oriented language) or the CDP1802 machine language. You can start with CHIP-8—a programming guide is included with the computer—after which you'll find machine language is easier to learn. CHIP-8 is an interpretive, hexadecimal language that you can learn very quickly. Each instruction consists of four hexadecimal digits. The first digit is the actual instruction, telling the VIP which of the machine-language subroutines to use. (Subroutines are sections of code that are executed repeatedly by a program. They can be thought of as blocks of instructions used in common by several different parts of a program.) The rest of the digits in a

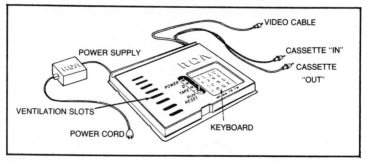

Fig. 6-98. Cosmac VIP-711 single-board computer. (Courtesy, RCA.)

CHIP-8 instruction give the VIP all the necessary information about the instruction, such as the values to use or the location where the values are stored.

This modular computer system can be expanded by the addition of a number of peripherals, as follows:

● **RAM on-board expansion kit** (expands the memory to 4K).

● **VP-570 Memory expander** (provides 4K of additional memory).

● **VP-575 system expansion board** (allows simultaneous use of up to 5 accessory boards, and up to 24K total RAM including the 4K on-board RAM); just plug in 5 VP-570 memory expansion boards, up to 20K of ROM; this can include the VP-700 Tiny BASIC in ROM board to allow programming with this high-level language, combinations of RAM and ROM, VP-

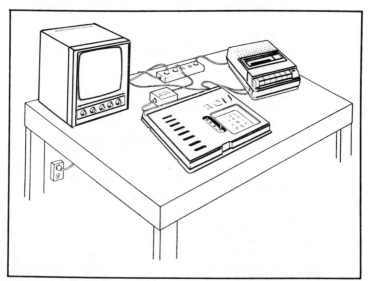

Fig. 6-99. Cosmac VIP-711 computer interconnected with television set and cassette player. (Courtesy, RCA.)

590 Color Board, other user-designed accessories or I/O ports for control applications.

- **VP-590 color display** (provides the added dimension of color).

- **VP-580 plus VP-585** (auxiliary keyboard and interface board adds two-player interactive capability. You can connect one or two of these 16-key hexadecimal keypads to your computer via sockets provided on either the companion VP-585 interface board or the VP-590 color display board).

- **Sound Boards.** (There are three sound boards: *VP-595 simple sound board*, which adds sound effects or mood melodies to the graphic display for added realism (256 programmable selectable tones; over four complete musical octaves); *VP-550 super sound board*, which effectively turns your computer into a music and sounds-effect device; you can compose your own music; while two separate sound channels make the computer sound like a two-piece combo; and *VP-551 four-channel super sound*; providing four-channel synthesis. Each channel can be programmed for frequency and note envelope independently; provides four-part harmony and the illusion of several instruments playing at once.

- **VP-3301 interactive data terminal** (microprocessor-based computer terminal with keyboard, video interface, and color graphics. Keyboard is 58-key typewriter-style board with upper- and lowercase characters. The display offers 24 lines by 40 characters in a 5×6 dot matrix, and you have a choice of 8 colors.

- **VP-601 keyboard** (see Fig. 6-100) (Board utilizes flexible membrane key switches with a light-positive action pressure. There are 58 alphabetic keys and 16 numeric/special control keys.)

Fig. 6-100. Keyboard that can be attached to a VP-7ll computer. (Courtesy, RCA.)

Fig. 6-101. VP-3301 microprocessor-controlled video terminal. (Courtesy, RCA.)

This keyboard can also be used as an interactive data terminal, which—connected to a television set and modem—can be used to access remote data bases or to create color graphics. In this configuration, the keyboard has been made programmable by adding a microprocessor, and is available as Model VP-3301 (Fig. 6-101). The data terminal creates 24 lines by 40 characters, software selectable. Each character or all characters may be displayed in any one of 8 colors.

ROCKWELL INTERNATIONAL SINGLE-BOARD

The AIM 65 shares many of the characteristics that bind this class of computers together: it's small, reasonably priced, and provides a remarkable vehicle for learning about computers and programming. It's a bit more difficult than other single-board computers of the same type, but its superb documentation offsets this problem.

Essentially, this is a single-board computer built around the 6502 microprocessor. A complete general-purpose microcomputer, it's ideal as an introduction to the world of microprocessing. (See Fig. 6-102.)

The unit—which comes complete with keyboard and printer—consists of two modules: the master module and the keyboard module, interconnected by a short plug-in ribbon cable. The master module holds a printer, a display and the microcomputer components (Fig. 6-103). The R6502 CPU has 56 instructions and 13 addressing modes, but is easy to program. The CPU can address 4K bytes of RAM and 20K bytes of ROM, plus an additional 40K bytes of user-provided external RAM, ROM, or I/O.

From Fig. 6-102, you can see the keyboard with 54 alphanumeric keys, providing 70 different alphabetic, numeric, control, and special functions. Located above the keyboard is a 20-character alphanumeric display. To the left of the display is a 120-line, 20-column (minimum) hard-copy printer. Behind the printer is the systems applications connector: this 44-pin connector lets you connect peripherals interfaced with I/O capabilities, such as one or two cassette recorders, a teletypewriter, and switches and sensors using serial and parallel TTL-level interfaces. (TTL stands for transistor-transistor logic.)

Behind the 6502 processor is a full-bus system expansion connector. This 44-pin connector extends address, data, and control bus; and lets you add on prototyping boards, PROM programmer, additional memory boards, floppy disc, modular modem analog interface boards, and other subsystem modules.

Fig. 6-102. AIM 65 single-board computer. (Courtesy, Rockwell International.)

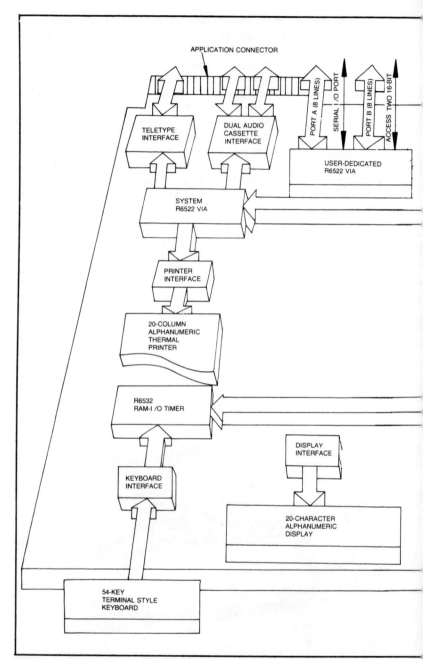

Fig. 6-103. Block diagram of AIM 65 single-board computer. (Courtesy, Rockwell International.)

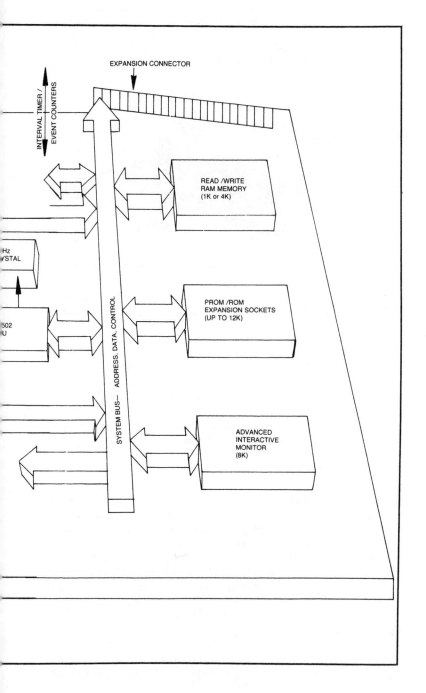

EXPANSION CONNECTOR

INTERVAL TIMER / EVENT COUNTERS

READ /WRITE RAM MEMORY (1K or 4K)

PROM /ROM EXPANSION SOCKETS (UP TO 12K)

ADVANCED INTERACTIVE MONITOR (8K)

SYSTEM BUS— ADDRESS. DATA. CONTROL

Hz CRYSTAL

6502 CPU

Fig. 6-104. Sinclair Z80 mini personal computer. (Courtesy, Sinclair Research Ltd.)

Going forward from this connector are the plug-in sockets for up to eight 4K bytes RAM memory devices. Next is the BASIC interpreter firmware, and next to this are five plug-in sockets for 4K byte ROM modules each. Next to the sockets are a symbolic assembler firmware and advanced interactive monitor firmware.

A number of compact, board-level products, available from Rockwell and other suppliers, provide the AIM 65 with design flexibility.

SINCLAIR RESEARCH LTD.

The Sinclair Z80 is a compact, briefcase-size computer weighing only 12 ounces. The computer is completely contained on a single circuit board sandwiched between a plastic case. Built around the Z-80 microprocessor, the plastic enclosure houses a 40-key, pressure-sensitive keyboard, built-in rf modulator, 1K bytes of RAM, 4K bytes of system ROM, and a cassette interface. (See Fig. 6-104.)

Supplied with a power supply and TV transfer switch, the unit sets up easily (Fig. 6-105). Because of its simplicity and price (under $200), the unit is ideal for those who want to get their feet wet operating a computer. An excellent manual guides you step by step through the programming sequences.

The black and white display (uppercase only), is limited to 24 lines by 32 characters, with 24 standard graphic symbols. Although at the time of this writing Sinclair has promised that 16K RAM and 8K ROM expansions will soon be available, the unit is not viable as a building block for a larger system. The computer has a 44-pin extension bus connector, but no suitable peripherals are presently available. However, as stated earlier, the Sinclair computer is a good choice for beginners.

TEXAS INSTRUMENTS INC.

In June 1979, Texas Instruments introduced its TI 99/4 personal computer. The TI 99/4 has a 40-key keyboard, 26K of internal ROM, and 16K of RAM. It's built around the TMS 9900 microprocessor (which is designed and manufactured by Texas Instruments), making it the only 16-bit personal/home computer. (See Fig. 6-106.) The system features color graphics, music capabilities, and programmable sound effects. ROM solid-state software modules may be plugged into a slot in the keyboard chassis (Fig. 6-107). The computer can address up to 72K of memory: 16K RAM, 26K of internal ROM, and up to 30K of ROM in the form of software modules.

The display generates 24 lines by 32 characters, uppercase only, in an 8×8 matrix. Sixteen colors are provided: white, gray, magenta, light yellow, yellow, light red, medium red, dark red, cyan, light blue, light green, medium green, dark green, black, transparent. A separate television set or monitor must be used. Set up and connections are simple.

Another capability of the computer is speech synthesis, by means of a solid-state synthesizer that comes equipped with a 200-word vocabulary, allowing you to have the computer give verbal prompts under program control.

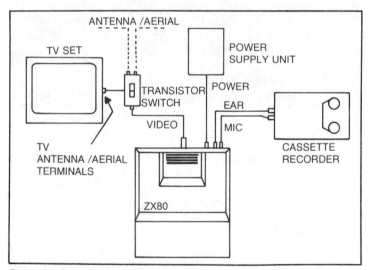

Fig. 6-105. Connecting the Z80 to TV and cassette recorder is a simple procedure accomplished in a matter of minutes. (Courtesy, Sinclair Research Ltd.)

Fig. 6-106. TI 99/4 personal/home computer connected to a television set. (Courtesy, Texas Instruments.)

The TI 99/4 is a modular, building-block type of system, meaning you can build the system up by adding the necessary peripherals and accessories. Figure 6-108 illustrates what the total system looks like.

Some peripherals are described below:

RS-232C Interface

This is a communications adapter that lets you connect a wide range of serially formatted accessory devices to the computer, including those from other manufacturers. (An exception is the modem, which must be the TI version.) With the RS-232C interface connected to the computer, you can list programs on a printer, send and receive data from a terminal, and so forth.

With the addition of the coupler (modem) you can communicate with other computers over the telephone lines. You can also access such data bases as The Source and CompuServe. The interface unit is programmable, to let you exchange data with a variety of serially formatted devices. Figure 6-109 shows the interface unit.

Telephone Coupler

This acoustic coupler, or modem, when connected to the interface unit, allows you to communicate with other computers and to access such data bases as The Source and CompuServe. (See Fig. 6-110.) The unit functions as a modulator to convert data you enter on your computer into signals that can be sent over the telephone lines. It also functions as a demodulator to convert data received over the phone lines back to its original form.

The unit has three controls: full-duplex operation—characters typed on keyboard are sent out without being displayed or printed; test—sets up audio self-test mode; and half-duplex (characters typed on keyboard are not only sent out, but also appear on your monitor or printer). The coupler can be set in either answer or originate mode. The data rate is 300 bits per second, and the unit is compatible with Bell 103. A software module is provided to simplify use of the coupler for data-base access.

Fig. 6-107. Software for the TI 99/4 consists of plug-in modules that are inserted in a slot at the right side of the keyboard. (Courtesy, Texas Instruments.)

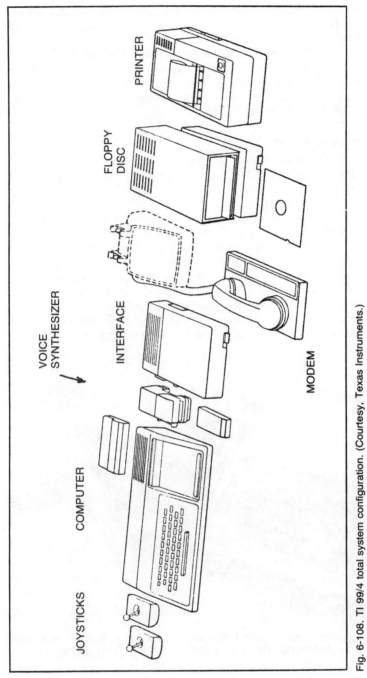

Fig. 6-108. TI 99/4 total system configuration. (Courtesy, Texas Instruments.)

JOYSTICKS

COMPUTER

VOICE
SYNTHESIZER

INTERFACE

MODEM

FLOPPY
DISC

PRINTER

Disc Memory Drive

This memory system allows you to store and retrieve data quickly on 5¼-in. discs. You can connect up to three floppy-disc drives to the TI 99/4 computer, via the disc-drive controller (Fig. 6-111, where the floppy disc is situated on top of the controller). There's storage of 90K bytes on each floppy disc.

The system includes floppy-disc drive(s) that can locate any position or file on the disc, as directed by the disc-drive controller. The drive spins the disc at a constant speed and controls the movement of the magnetic head. A controller tells the disc drive where to position the magnetic head in order to read or write information properly. The controller also puts an index on the disc, making the data that has been written easy to locate. A software module helps you maintain the information on your discs. Naming and renaming discs, renaming files, deleting files, copying files, and copying discs—all can be easily performed with the software program.

Fig. 6-109. Interface RS-232C allows the use of various peripherals, such as modem, printer, and disc drives. (Courtesy, Texas Instruments.)

Fig. 6-110. Acoustic coupler, or modem, allows communication between other computers as well as access to remote data bases. (Courtesy, Texas Instruments.)

Thermal Printer

This is a quiet, smooth-running electronic printing device. When connected to the computer, it can provide a printed copy of your program as well as data to aid you in revising long programs or maintaining files of programs and results. Software modules are available to print screen displays. (See Fig. 6-112.)

The thermal printer contains a stepper motor that moves heat-sensitive (thermal) paper past stationary electronic printheads. The roller moves in tiny steps; between each step, small semiconductor elements are heated by electronic circuits, producing data on the thermal paper. After several steps, these dots form numbers, letters, and symbols on paper. The printer prints about 30 characters per second, 32 characters on a line; it has 32 graphic symbols in a predefined set of 128 characters, and prints upper- and lowercase characters.

Solid-State Speech Synthesizer

This exciting device adds the dimension of voice to the TI 99/4 computer. Completely electronic, without taped voice recordings or other traditional recording media, the synthesizer contains a vocabulary of more than 300 words. Plug-in software speech modules can add another 800 words. The unit simply connects to the computer by means of a built-in connector.

Speech is generated by inserting a module such as the Speech Editor, that's programmed for speech. All words and phrases are permanently filed in memory chips stored in the synthesizer. Each word has been transformed

Fig. 6-111. Floppy-disc drive is shown situated on top of controller, with disc in front. (Courtesy, Texas Instruments.)

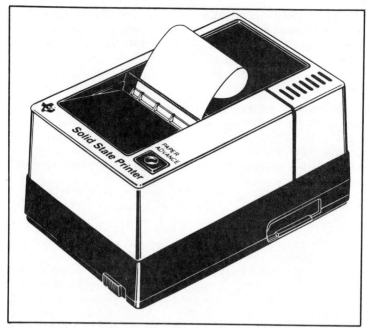

Fig. 6-112. Thermal printer used with TI 99/4 computer. (Courtesy, Texas Instruments.)

into a pattern of bits stored in the circuitry. This rebuilds the requested word, and audibly reproduces a voice through the speaker in the monitor or television set.

By combining the Speech Editor software module and the synthesizer, you have access to two modes of speech generation: direct speech construction and editing, via the keyboard and monitor; and through the TI BASIC language with special verbs for speech output. Using the speech construction method, you can type on the keyboard the words or sentences to be recited. They're displayed on the screen, and played back through the speaker. This feature, which requires no programming knowledge to use, lets you try out various words and phrases in real time.

Implementing CALL SAY (one of the BASIC subprograms in the second-access mode), words, phrases or sentences may be recited under program control—that is, you can program your own words and sentences.

Many words in the English language are pronounced similarly but spelled differently; these are called *homonyms*. Other words are pronounced differently but spelled the same; these are called *homographs*. The synthesizer has both in its vocabulary.

Example of homonyms are TO, TWO, TOO, and 2. The synthesizer recognizes these different ways of spelling words that sound the same. Homographs pose an altogether different problem. Since spellings are identical, the computer can't tell which pronunciation is wanted. Therefore, to differentiate between two pronunciations a number is placed immediately after one of the homographs. For example, READ is pronounced "red," like reed; READ1 is pronounced "red," like the color red. In its list of words, Texas Instruments lists these homographs and their designations with "1".

The list of available software is also impressive. Some subjects:

Household Budget Management. Helps families implement a budget and monitor their expenses by category, month, and year. It can assist you to foresee the effects of new purchases, or of changes in income or expenses. It can also help project cash position—something especially important when new purchases are being considered. Charts and graphics help you quickly pinpoint dangerous expenses and trends.

Home Financial Decisions. A valuable tool in helping people make intelligent decisions about loans, housing, automobiles, and savings. Helps you explore available alternatives, by asking straightforward questions. Sophisticated cash-flow models analyze these situations with depth and insight. This program also helps you to take the guesswork out of such questions as: Should I lease or buy a car? Is it more advantageous to buy a home or to rent? Should I keep my current house or buy a new one? Is one house a better investment than another? Should I pay off a certain loan early?

Beginning Grammar. This helps children in the grades 3 through 5 learn the basic parts of speech.

Early Learning Fun. This "learning by doing" program combines shape, number, and letter recognition activities with exercises in counting and sorting. This is an excellent entry point into the computer world, since it teaches children the basic keyboard functions and the fun of interacting with a computer.

Number Magic. For elementary-age children 5 and up. This math education program helps teach addition, subtraction, multiplication, and division by means of a series of easy-to-follow, gamelike activities.

Physical Fitness. This program assists you in developing a custom exercise plan based on age and general fitness. It contains five progressive exercise levels, with separate categories for men and women. The computer helps you to stick with the program selected by setting the cadence and number of repetitions for each exercise, and by setting the proper warm-up/cool-down sequences.

Video Chess. This program allows you to play chess, either against the computer or against another opponent.

Football. A program based on football play probabilities, based on actual professional statistics. A two-player game.

Video Graphs. This program uses the system's color- and pattern-generating capabilities in an exciting way. You can create fine-line drawings, design beautiful mosaic patterns, or construct colorful pictures built of geometric video building blocks. Any pattern or picture generated can be stored for future review or rework.

Statistics. Provides a library of established routines for persons with some previous statistical experience.

Personal Record Keeping. This handy program offers a computerized solution for generating, maintaining, and manipulating a filing system. You determine the files to be collected; you can include such items as mailing lists, household inventory, stamp or coin collections, and recipes. Once you have your files established, the computer makes it easy to rearrange the contents, display selected lists, and analyze relationships between items.

Securities Analysis. Provides a financial package for the home-computer user seeking assistance in evaluation, selection, and management of his or her investment portfolio.

Speech Editor. (Described earlier.)

Early Reading. Teaches pre-school children to associate graphic images with printed and spoken words. Utilizes the speech synthesizer.

Glossary

access time—The time required for the computer to move data between its memory and its CPU.

acoustic coupler—Variety of modem that uses a conventional handset.

address—A number used by the CPU to specify a location in memory.

alphanumeric—Describes a set of characters containing single-digit numbers and the letters of the alphabet, along with punctuation marks and symbols.

ALU—Arithmetic and logic unit; that part of the CPU that executes, adds, subtracts, shifts and logic operations, or logic operations.

applications software—Software programs written to perform particular functions, such as home budgets, home security control, etc.

assembler—Software that converts the assembly language of a computer program into the machine language of the computer.

assembly language—Grouped alphabetic characters, called *mnemonics*, that replace the numeric instructions of machine language.

asynchronous transmission—Data transmission in which each character has its own start and stop bits, and there's no control over the time between characters.

BASIC—Beginner's All-Purpose Symbolic Instruction Code. A simplified programming language.

baud rate—A measure of the rate of data flow between any two devices. Specifies how many units of information can be transmitted along a telephone line in a second. The higher the baud rate, the higher the speed of transmission.

binary—Refers to a numbering system consisting of only two digits, 1 and 0. The words *binary, two-state*, and *digital* are synonymous.

bipolar—Said of transistors in which the working current flows through two types of semiconductor material, called N-type and P-type; current consists of both positive and negative electrical charges.

bit—Smallest unit of information a computer deals with. A bit can have one of two values, 1 or 0.

bus—A group of wires that allows memory, CPU, and I/O services to exchange.

byte—A string of 8 bits. A byte is the amount of storage space needed to represent a character. Kilobyte [K]= 1,000 bytes; megabyte [M]= 1 million bytes.

carrier signal—A signal that contains no information by itself, but whose characteristics can be altered to carry data.

chip—A thin silicon wafer on which electronic components are deposited in the form of integrated circuits.

clock—An electronic circuit that generates timing pulses to synchronize the operation of a computer.

command—A request to the computer that is executed as soon as it has been received.

compiler—A program that translates the high-level language statements of a program into machine-readable form.

CPU—Central processing unit; the part of the computer that performs calculations and processes data according to the instructions specified by the software.

CRT—Cathode-ray tube; a video screen that displays prompting instructions, user responses, and reports generated by the computer.

cursor—A symbol placed on the screen to indicate where the next character will appear.

digital signal—A signal that takes on two distinct values representing binary 0s and 1s.

disc[ette]—A revolving plate upon which data and programs are stored.

disc drive—A piece of hardware that houses several magnetic discs; it keeps them spinning so that information can be read from or stored on the discs.

DOS—Disk operating system; a collection of programs that facilitate the use of the disc drive.

dot-matrix display—A display format consisting of small light-emitting elements arranged as a matrix. Various elements are energized to depict a character.

dual-density—Refers to a means of storing data on a disc at twice the density that was formerly standard.

FET—Field-effect transistor; a monolithic semiconductor amplifying device in which a high impedance gate electrode controls the flow of current carried through a thin bar of silicon called the channel; its internal operation is unipolar in nature.

fetch—Reading out an instruction at a particular memory location into the CPU.

firmware—The part of a computer program that is incorporated as machine hardware—for example, instructions contained in ROM.

floppy disc—Inexpensive magnetic storage medium that uses disc[ettes].

frequency modulation—Common method of transferring data via modem, in which the frequency (pitch or tone) of a carrier signal is altered to represent digital data's 1s and 0s.

full duplex—Simultaneous, independent transmission of data in both directions over a communications line.

half duplex—Operation of a communications link in either direction over a single channel, but not in both directions simultaneously.

hard copy—Printed copy of computer output.

hard disc—Similar to a floppy disc, but larger and not flexible. Hard discs hold more data and allow for higher access speeds, but are more expensive.

High-Level Language—Programming language containing statements in English that are translated by the computer's compiler into machine language.

instruction—A group of bits that defines a computer operation. An instruction may move data, do arithmetic and logic functions, control I/O devices, or make decisions as to which instruction to execute next.

interface—The hardware for linking two units of electronic equipment—as a computer with input or output device.

interpreter—A program that translates each of the statements of a high-level language into machine language as they're entered on the keyboard. An interpreter is generally used with BASIC.

I/O—Input/output; used to describe equipment designed to communicate with the computer.

k—Quantity of 1,000, approximately (actually 1,024).

language—The method or technique used to instruct a computer to perform various operations.

LCD—Liquid-crystal display; a liquid crystal hermetically sealed between two glass plates.

LED—Light-emitting diode; a semiconductor device that gives off light when current passes through it.

light pen—A light-sensitive device used with a computer-operated CRT display for selecting a portion of the display for action by the computer.

machine language—A program consisting of a string of 1s and 0s that the computer understands directly.

memory—Part of the central processing unit that holds information being processed.

menu—A list of alternative actions displayed on the screen for selection by the user.

microprocessor—The semiconductor chip that serves as the core of the central processing unit.

mnemonic code—Instructions for a computer written in a form that is easy for the computer to remember. Mnemonic-code programs must always be converted to machine language.

modem—A device that couples a computer or terminal to a telephone line.

modulation—The process of altering the tone, volume, or rhythm of a carrier signal to convey information.

MOS—Metal oxide semiconductor; technology used to produce the microprocessor and memory portions of computers.

network—A system of interconnected computers and/or terminals.

operating system—A series of programs, generally provided by the manufacturer as part of the computer system, that controls the physical operation of the computer, such as printing and accepting input from the keyboard.

originate/answer—Two modes of operation of a modem. In the originate mode, the modem will utilize one set of frequencies to transmit data and another set of frequencies to receive data. In the answer mode, these frequency sets are reversed. In order for two modems to communicate, one modem must be in the originate mode and the other in the answer mode.

peripherals—Input, output, and data-storage devices such as printers, keyboards, CRTs, and tape and disc drives.

phase modulation—A method of transferring data via modem in which the rhythm of a carrier signal is altered to represent digital 1s and 0s.

port—Portion of the computer through which a peripheral can communicate.

program—A set of coded instructions directing a computer to perform a particular function.

PROM—Programmable ROM; can be programmed by the user, but only once. After a PROM has been programmed, it becomes a ROM.

pulse—An abrupt change in voltage that conveys digital information over a circuit.

RAM—Random-access memory; a read/write memory that stores information in such a way that each bit of information may be retrieved within the same amount of time as any other bit.

read/write memory—Memory whose contents can be continuously changed, quickly and easily, during system operation.

real time—Pertains to the performance of a computation during the actual time that the related physical process occurs, so that results of the computation can be used to guide the physical process.

ROM—Read-only memory; if RAM is like a scratch pad, then ROM is like a printed book whose pages cannot be erased. System software is often stored in ROM.

save—To store a program somewhere other than in the computer's memory—as on disc or tape.

semiconductor—A material with a conductivity between that of a metal and an insulator—usually silicon. Used in diodes, transistors, and integrated circuits.

simplex—A communications link capable of transmitting data in only one direction.

software—Programs or instructions that tell the computer how to respond to specific commands.

synchronous transmission—Data transmission in which the bits are transmitted at a fixed rate.

systems software—Software programs that control the internal operations of the computer, such as the translation of keyboard commands into a form that can be acted upon by the CPU.

terminal—A peripheral device through which information is entered into or extracted from the computer.

time sharing—The simultaneous use of a computer by two or more parties from separate, remote terminals.

unipolar—Describes transistors in which the working current flows through only one kind of semiconductor material, either N-type or P-type.

utility program—Software that performs such frequently required processes as sorting, deleting, and copying.

Appendix: Computer Specifications

COMPUTER	MICROPROCESSOR DEVICE	BITS	RAM (BYTES) STD.	MAX.	ROM (BYTES) STD.	MAX.	OPERATING SYSTEM	PROGRAM LANGUAGE	VIDEO DISPLAY TERMINAL PACKAGE	CHARACT.	GRAPHICS	COLORS	INPUT/OUTPUT SERIAL I/O	MODEM	PRINTER	LIGHT PEN	HAND CONTROLS	MASS STORAGE CASSETTE	FLOPPY STD. PKG.	BYTES MAX.	REMARKS
APF ELECTRONICS IMAGINATION MACHINE	MC6800	8	9K	8K (24K #II)	14K	14K	Lvel I BAS.	BASIC	Video Mon.	16×32	256×192	8	Optional	Optional	Optional	-	Included	Included	Optional	140K	53-key keyboard 3 octaves
APPLE COMPUTERS APPLE II	6502	8	16K	64K	16K	16K	DOS 3.3	BASIC	TV/Mon.	24×40	193×280	15	Optional	None	Optional	Optional	Included	Optional	Optional	560K	51-key / 4 octaves
APPLE II PLUS	6502	8	16K	64K	16K	16K	DOS 3.3	BASIC	TV/Mon.	24×40	193×280	15	Optional	None	Optional	Optional	Included	Optional	Optional	560K	51-key / 4 octaves
APPLE II	6502	8	96K	128K	4K	4K	SOS	BASIC/Pas	Video Mon.	24×80	192×280	16	Std.	Optional	Optional	-	Optional	None	140K	560K	74-key / 4 octaves
ASTROVISION BALLY ARCADE	Z-80	8	32K	64K	16K	16K	B. BASIC	Zgrass B.	TV/Mon.	NA	100×160	256	Std.	Optional	Optional	Optional	Included	Included	-	-	NA / 3 octaves
ATARI COMPUTERS 400	6502	8	8K	16K	10K	10K	BASIC	BASIC	TV/Mon.	24×40	192×320	16	Std.	Optional	Optional	Optional	Included	Optional	-	-	61-key / 4 octaves
800	6502	8	16K	48K	10K	10K	BASIC	BASIC	TV/Mon.	24×40	192×320	16	Std.	Optional	Optional	Optional	Included	Optional	88K	352K	61-key / 4 octaves
CASIO FX-900P	8080	8	4K	20K	4K	NA	NA	NA	TV/Mon.	16×32	128×256	NA	NA	NA	NA	NA	NA	NA	NA	NA	NA
COMMODORE BUS.MACH PET 2001	6502	8	8K	32K	14K	22K	BASIC	BASIC	Built-in	25×40	128×192	16	Std.	Optional	Optional	Optional	Optional	Optional	170K	512K	84-key
VIC 20	6502	8	5K	32K	-	27K	BASIC	BASIC	TV/Mon.	22×23	176×176	16	Std.	None	Optional	Optional	Optional	Optional	-	-	66-key / 3 octaves
COMPUCOLOR II																					
EXIDY INC. SORCERER II	Z-80	8	32K	48K	16K	48K	BASIC	BASIC	Monitor	30×65	240×512	2	Std.	Optional	Included	None	None	Optional	Optional	1000K	65-key
HEWLETTE-PACKARD	NMOS	8	16K	32K	32K	48K	BASIC	BASIC	Monitor	16×32	256×192	16	Std.	Optional	Optional	None	None	Included	Std.	4720K	92-key

COMPUTER	MICROPROCESSOR		RAM (BYTES)		ROM (BYTES)		OPERATING PROGRAM		VIDEO DISPLAY TERMINAL				INPUT / OUTPUT					MASS STORAGE			REMARKS
	DEVICE	BITS	STD.	MAX.	STD.	MAX.	SYSTEM	LANGUAGE	PACKAGE	CHARACT.	GRAPHICS	COLORS	SERIAL I/O	MODEM	PRINTER	LIGHT PEN	HAND CONTROLS	CASSETTE	FLOPPY BYTES STD	FLOPPY BYTES PKG.	
IBM	8080	16	16K	256K	40K	40K	IBM DOS	BASIC	Intel	25×80	320×200	16	Std.	Optional	Optional	Optional	Optional	Optional	320K	320K	83-key
INTERTEC DATA SYST. SUPERBRAIN	Z-80A	8	32K	64K	2K	2K	CP /M	BASIC	Included	25×80	NA	NA	Std.	Optional	Optional	NA	NA	-	350K	700K	NA
MATTEL ELECTR. INTELLIVISION	6502	16	16K	8MB	10K	10K	BASIC	BASIC	TV /Mon.	25×40	160×192	16	Std.	Optional	Optional	Optional	Included	Included	-	-	60-key / 3 octaves
NIPPON ELECTRIC CO. NEC-8001	Z-80 comp.	8	32K	160K	24K	32K	NA	BASIC	TV /Mon.	25×80	160×100	8	Std.	Optional	Optional	-	-	Optional	143K	286K	82-key
OHIO SCIENTIFIC INC. C1P C4P C8P	6502 6502 6502	8 8 8	8K 24K 48K	32K 24K 48K	10K 10K 10K	10K 10K 10K	OS-DOS OS-DOS OS-DOS	BASIC BASIC BASIC	TV /Mon. TV /Mon. TV /Mon.	24×24 32×64 32×64	256×256 256×512 256×512	2 15 15	Std. Std. Std.	Optional Optional Optional	Optional Optional Optional	- - -	Optional Optional Optional	Optional Optional Optional	None 80K 250K	180K 80K 250K	53-key / 6 octaves 53-key / 6 octaves 53-key / 6 octaves
PANASONIC HHC	6502	8	2K	4K	16K	64K	NA	BASIC	TV /Mon.	16×24	48×64	8	NA	Optional	Optional	NA	NA	Optional	NA	NA	65-key

COMPUTER	MICROPROCESSOR		RAM (BYTES)		ROM (BYTES)		OPERATING SYSTEM	PROGRAM LANGUAGE	INPUT/OUTPUT										MASS STORAGE			REMARKS
									VIDEO DISPLAY TERMINAL				SERIAL I/O	MODEM	PRINTER	LIGHT PEN	HAND CONTROLS		CASSETTE	FLOPPY BYTES		
	DEVICE	BITS	STD.	MAX.	STD.	MAX.			PACKAGE	CHARACT.	GRAPHICS	COLORS								STD. PKG.	MAX.	
PERSONAL MICRO COMP. PMC-80	Z-80	8	16K	48K	12K	12K	BASIC	BASIC	TV/Mon.	16×64	128×48	-	Std.	Optional	Optional	Optional	Optional	Built-in	-	-	-
RADIO SHACK TRS-80/I	Z-80	8	16K	48K	12K	12K	TRS DOS	BASIC	Included	16×32	128×48	-	Std	Optional	Optional	Optional	-	-	Optional	86K	53-key
TRS-80/II	Z-80	8	32K	64K	12K	12K	TRS DOS	BASIC	Included	24×80	128×48	-	Std	Optional	Optional	-	-	-	416K	2MB	76-key
TRS-80/III	Z-80	8	4K	48K	4K	14K	TRS DOS	BASIC	Included	16×64	128×48	-	Optional	Optional	Optional	-	-	Optional	156K	617K	65-key
TRS-80/COLOR	6809E	8	4K	20K	8K	8K	TRS DOS	BASIC	Optional	16×32	32×64	8	Std.	Optional	Optional	-	Optional	Optional	-	-	53-key
HHC	CMOS CDP	4	1.9K	1.9K	11K	11K	BASIC	BASIC	None	1×24	N/A	-	-	-	Std.	-	-	Optional	-	-	53-key
RCA	1802	8	2K	24K	4K	20K	CDP1802	Chip-8	Optional	24×40	-	6	Optional	Optional	Optional	-	-	-	-	-	74-key
SHARP ELECTR. PC-1211	CMOS	4	1.9K	1.9K	11K	11K	BASIC	BASIC	None	1×24	-	-	-	-	Optional	-	Optional	Optional	-	-	53-key
SINCLAIR ZX-80	Z-80	8	1K	17K	4K	12K	BASIC	BASIC	TV/Mon.	24×32	-	-	-	-	-	-	-	Optional	-	-	40-key
TEXAS INSTRUMENTS 99/4	TMS9900	16	16K	48K	26K	30K	TI BASIC	BASIC	TV/Mon.	24×32	192×256	16	Optional	Optional	Optional	-	Optional	Optional	90K	270K	40-key/5 octaves

Index

30124 75152 42061

JACK PALMER

31-12-81